Dear Social

Dear Social Media Manager

Advice, tips and truths from those who know the industry best.

Xandrina Allday

Copyright © 2024 Xandrina Allday

All rights reserved

I dedicate this book to all social media professionals, past, present and future.

I hope that the letters in this book inspire and motivate you today and throughout your career in social media.

Contents

Acknowledgements..1
Preface..3
Introduction...5
Adina Jipa...8
Alexus Brittain...10
Andrea Kilin..12
Anna Bertoldini..14
Anna Wamsler..16
Anthony Leung...18
Carolyn Campbell-Baldwin....................................20
Corrie Jones..22
Dave Endsor..24
Diana Rapine...26
Dynamitri Joachim..28
Emma Glover...30
Fab Giovanetti...32
Grace Clemens..34
Grace Mcglaughlin..36
Gus Bhandal..38
Holly Hammond...40
James Erskine..42
Joe Teo...44
Jonathan Hatch..46
Karla McNeilage...48
Kate Berry...50
Katie Murphy...52
Kim Stavropoulos..54
Lauren Grubb..56
Lena Weber-Reed...58
Magali Mas D'Amato...60
Maja Ivic...62
Mandie Gellar..64
Mandy Karl...66
Marianne Avery..68
Mariya Spektor...70
Mark Valasik..72
Matt Swain..74
Mike Allton...76

Miruna Vocheci	78
Nick Entwistle	80
Paige F.Macgregor	82
Patricia Fernandes	84
Rebecca Holloway	86
Sabreen Haziq	88
Sarah Clay	90
Sree Sreenavisan	92
Tania Gerard	94
Tara Jabbari	96
Xandrina Allday	98
Contributors	101
About The Author	114

Acknowledgements

Dear Social Media Manager was inspired by the incredible social media community that I have found myself a part of online and in person. It is this community that I wanted to share as far and as wide as possible. It has given me the greatest joy to write, compile and edit this book.

I would like to thank the following for their advice, support and contributions throughout the years and this book, whom without this wouldn't have been created:

My family, Darren, Piper and Blake, who love and support me every day, they are my biggest advocates and motivation. I wouldn't be me without them.

Stacey Fordham-Gray was working in social media long before myself, she unknowingly made me realise that social media was a career that I wanted to pursue. This book is the definition of the butterfly effect.

Lucy Hall's event SocialDay, is what sparked the fire inside me to create something for the social media community, in the form of this book.

Kirstie Cartledge and the rest of the Webcertain team for quite literally giving me the stage and connecting me to so many wonderful social media professionals at the International Social Media Summit 2024.

Ash Board who's had a huge impact on my career, in which he has challenged, encouraged and motivated me to become better at my job and as a team leader too.

Matt Navarra has been a constant resource throughout my time working in social media, for which without I would have even less hours in the day.

To my social media spice girls:

Abi-Bellion Carey is an incredible speaker in the social media industry, she's who gave me the confidence and inspiration I needed to start speaking on stages at events both online and in real life.

Annie-Mai Hodge is the Founder of Girl Power Marketing, I will always be in awe of the community that she has built. Not only is she an absolute powerhouse in the social media industry, she's my soundboard for any opinions I have that go against the grain.

Rebecca Holloway is one to watch in social media, she's a fellow Author and I'm so grateful for her wisdom and endless support in such a short time of knowing one another.

The incredible social media professionals who have contributed to this book, whom without none of this would be possible. I'm truly grateful to each and every one of you for being involved with this project.

To you the reader, I'm so pleased you decided to read Dear Social Media Manager. I truly hope this has an impact on you and becomes a resource you turn to time and time again.

Preface

For as long as I can remember, I've always wanted to be an Author, but it always felt like a bit of a pipedream. I've thought of multiple concepts for books, spanning topics like social media to motivation to grief. However interestingly, Dear Social Media Manager is the most recent idea I came up with and I decided to make this idea into a reality sooner rather than later.

The further I progress in my career and the more I lean into the social media industry and community as a whole, the more I fall in love with what I do (what we all do). The social media community is unbelievably supportive, it's full of inspiring, creative and smart individuals, who collectively are the voices behind brands all around the world.

When attending social media events in person or online, we become connected with other social media professionals. It's at these events that you really feel that sense of community and gain that peer support, that as individuals you may not have on a day-to-day basis. Not to mention all the learnings and takeaways you come away with and can action thereafter. I will always be the biggest advocate for attending events, but I may be slightly biassed as my career started in events management before pivoting to working in marketing. However, I truly believe events can reignite your passion and creativity working in social media.

It was in the week between speaking at both SocialDay and the International Social Media Summit where the concept of this book came to me. I wanted to bottle the feeling I get at these events and the only way to do that is to hear from fellow social media managers, sharing their perspectives on their careers and the industry as a whole.

Whether you've been working in social media for 1 week or over

7 years like myself, or perhaps you just want to get a better understanding of the social media industry, this book will provide you with so many takeaways and I hope it makes you feel something too. If you've not felt like part of a community until this point, I hope this will open your eyes to how welcoming it truly is. You already know how important communities are because you (probably) work in social, but have you stopped to consider how important this is for yourself? Having a support network to lean on for both the good and bad days, is an essential part of your social media manager toolkit and I'm so happy to provide that for you in the form of this book.

Not only are there limited books in social media due to how quickly things evolve, but none of them really share the point of view from multiple social media professionals and I felt this was something that was missing from the social media industry.

Dear Social Media Manager is a conglomeration of letters from social media professionals. You may recognise some of the names who have contributed to the book and there will be many you've not heard of previously and that's the point. It represents the industry as a whole. Contributors have varying years of experience working in social media, some are brand side, others at agencies, some of them are freelancers and others employed.

I truly hope that this book resonates for you and if it does, please recommend it to another Social Media Manager and get a copy to your C-suite executives too. Together we can change our industry for the better and it starts with me and you.

Introduction

Social media evolves at a rapid pace. Social Media Managers are the ones who have to adapt on a daily basis to platform updates, trends and best practices. It's a mammoth task in itself but it makes the job fulfilling and rewarding both personally and professionally.

The Importance of Social Media
Social media is the amplification of every brand voice online. Social media is where people go to connect, relax, unwind, shop, communicate, be inspired, entertained and educated. Social media should never be an afterthought, arguably it should be one of the first marketing methods considered for any campaign, messaging or community building. Social media is brand marketing.

The Impact of Social Media on Search
The way we search has changed significantly since the creation of the internet. Social media platforms are becoming search engines in their own right. Emarketer reported "over half (51%) of Gen Z consumers worldwide use social media to look up a brand versus 45% who turn to search engines, per GWI Core data from 2023.", this highlights the importance of having an established social media strategy and a team in place to support these efforts.

Social Media Marketing is in Demand
LinkedIn's 2024 Global Marketing Jobs Outlook Research Report shared that the "most in-demand marketing skill of the moment is social media marketing", which is no surprise when you consider the above. However, in contrast it's an industry that is still undervalued and underpaid, which is often called out by social media professionals on LinkedIn. The fact these two things co-exist at the same time shows that education is still needed for wider understanding of the social media industry.

Reoccurring Themes

Dear Social Media Manager aims to shine a spotlight on the role Social Media Managers have not only in the social media industry but across companies globally. It shares the highs and lows, challenges and opportunities of working in the role, common pitfalls, career advice and how the social media landscape has changed over the years.

There are themes and ideas throughout the book that appear frequently, showing the prevalence of them.

Depending on your knowledge of social media when reading the book, depends on whether these things will surprise you or whether they will challenge or confirm your opinions. Dear Social Media Manager is here to enrich your understanding of the social media industry and the roles of social media managers and professionals within it.

Dear Social Media Manager:

A collection of letters written by social media professionals, sharing advice, tips and truths about the social media industry.

Dear Social Media Manager,

I hope this letter finds you well. I wanted to take this opportunity to discuss an important topic that affects many of us in the industry - social media measurement blind spots.

As Social Media Managers, we are constantly striving to understand and improve our strategies, but there are several blind spots that can hinder our progress.

One common blind spot is not having enough data to make informed decisions. On the contrary, having an overwhelming amount of data can also be problematic, leading to confusion and inefficiency.

Furthermore, failing to correlate data with industry insights or competitive research can prevent us from gaining a comprehensive understanding of our performance.

In addition, not knowing how to interpret the data, as well as not tracking the right metrics, can interfere with our efforts to evaluate the success of our campaigns effectively.

Moreover, understanding the customer journey and where social media impacts the buying journey is crucial, yet it's often overlooked. Many of us face challenges due to budget constraints, making it difficult to invest in enterprise-level tools and resources.

Lastly, not having the right person in our team to analyse the data can pose a significant obstacle to our measurement efforts.

I understand that navigating these blind spots can be daunting, especially for those new to the industry or for seasoned professionals looking to enhance their knowledge.

Dear Social Media Manager

It's important to acknowledge these challenges openly, as it creates a space for meaningful discussions and shared learnings within our community. I believe that by addressing and overcoming these blind spots, we can collectively elevate the social media industry and our own professional growth.

It's essential to approach these challenges with a positive mindset and a willingness to learn and adapt. Together, we can work towards improving our measurement strategies and achieving greater success in our roles as social media managers.

I hope this letter serves as a valuable reflection on the intricacies of social media measurement, and I encourage you to share your insights and experiences with your peers.

Let's continue to support one another in our journey to success in the dynamic world of social media.

Adina Jipa
Founder & CMO at Socialinsider

Dear Social Media Manager,

This field, while immensely rewarding, is also filled with challenges that test our resilience and creativity.

One of the most exhilarating aspects of our work is the unparalleled creative freedom we enjoy. The digital canvas is vast and ever-evolving, allowing us to craft compelling narratives, build vibrant communities, and engage audiences in ways that were truly unimaginable just a few years ago. This freedom is a testament to our role as innovators and storytellers in the digital age.

However, with this freedom comes the reality that our authority is often questioned. Despite our expertise and dedication, social media managers frequently find themselves at the bottom of the totem pole. Our strategic insights and hard work can be overlooked, and we sometimes face scepticism about the value we bring to the table.

Let's not let this be a source of discouragement. Instead, let's let it fuel our determination to prove our worth. We are professionals with a deep understanding of the digital landscape, a keen sense for trends, and a talent for connecting with audiences. OUR role is crucial, and the impact of our work is profound. Embrace this challenge as an opportunity to showcase skills and demonstrate the power of effective social media management.

It's also worth noting that the position we hold is relatively new. Not too long ago, the role of a social media manager didn't even exist. Today, almost every company and business recognises the necessity of having someone in this role (Ironic to my previous point, right?) This shift speaks volumes about the value and importance of our work. We are at the forefront of a digital revolution, shaping the way brands communicate and interact with their audiences.

Looking ahead to the future of social I truly believe that Social Media Managers are the next Chief Marketing Officers of the marketing world. As we continue to push through the noise and prove our strategic importance, we are paving the way for greater recognition and influence within our organizations. The skills we hone and the insights we provide are pivotal to the success of modern marketing strategies.

So, stay positive and uplifted. The path ahead is challenging, but it is also immensely rewarding. Our work matters, and our contributions are vital to the growth and success of the organizations we work for. Continue to innovate, inspire, and lead with confidence. Together, we are shaping the future of marketing, one post at a time.

Alexus Brittain
Head of Social Media at Vista Social

Dear Social Media Manager,

Welcome to the whirlwind world of social media! Whether you're just starting your journey or have already navigated its many twists and turns, there's always something new to learn in this ever-evolving industry. As someone who's about spent about 10 years in the trenches, I'm excited to share some insights, advice, and a few truths to help you on your path.

What I wish I knew before starting
When I first dove into social media, I underestimated the strategy involved. I loved creating the content, planning "the grid" on Instagram, picking a filter to make the algorithm like me, and making sure I have the minimum three posts a day on Twitter. I now understand that social media is more than posting updates and responding to comments; it's about understanding your audience, crafting compelling narratives, and measuring impact through analytics. If I could go back, I'd tell my younger self to embrace the analytical side of the job earlier. Learning to interpret metrics and adjust strategies is crucial for driving meaningful engagement.

Tips for Success:
1. Stay curious and keep learning: The platforms and best practices are always changing. Make a habit of staying updated with the latest trends and algorithm updates. Follow industry leaders, attend webinars, and don't be afraid to experiment.
2. Engage authentically: Authenticity is key in building a loyal following. Engage with your audience in a genuine way—listen to their feedback, respond thoughtfully, and show that there's a real person behind the brand.
3. Prioritise mental health: The 24/7 nature of social media can be overwhelming. Set boundaries to prevent burnout—schedule your posts, take regular breaks, and don't be afraid to unplug outside of work hours. Remember, your well-being is important too (I learnt this the hard way, twice).

The joys and challenges
Working in social media offers a unique blend of creativity and community. There's immense satisfaction in seeing your content resonate with people, sparking conversations, and building a brand's online presence. However, the job isn't without its challenges. The rapid pace and constant demand for content can be stressful. Negative feedback and online trolls are part of the landscape, and it's essential to develop a thick skin and a constructive approach to criticism.

Industry insights
The social media industry is a dynamic and exciting place, but it's also one that demands adaptability. User behavior changes, and platforms evolve. Flexibility and resilience are your best allies. Embrace the uncertainty, stay agile, and always be ready to pivot your strategies. Follow reputable publications and thought leaders to have access to news asap – not because you have to jump on the new platform, but to have the information to decide if it is a fit for your strategy.

Final thoughts
Despite the challenges, working in social media is incredibly rewarding. The ability to shape narratives, engage with diverse audiences, and drive real-world impact is powerful. Cherish the creative freedom and the opportunities to innovate. As you continue on this journey, remember that your work has the potential to make a difference—both for the brands you represent and the communities you engage with. Best of luck on your social media adventures!

Andrea Kilin
Social Media Director at Cytiva
Disclaimer: This text has been written with aid from generative AI.

Dear Social Media Manager,

So, you decided to embark on this new journey working in social media.

I'm excited for you. This dynamic function will offer you endless opportunities for creativity, growth, and impact. As someone who's worked with social media for nearly 7 years, I wanted to share some of what I learned, hoping it can help you too.

Staying relevant in the fast-paced world of social media can be demanding. Trends come and go at lightning speed, and keeping up can feel overwhelming. Stay updated with industry news, follow top influencers, engage people as ambassadors, and interact with your audience to stay relevant. Social networks evolve quickly, but this keeps you learning and adapting.

Creativity and innovation are the lifeblood of this job. You'll need to constantly brainstorm and experiment with new content ideas to captivate your audience. This can be a challenge, especially when inspiration runs dry, but it's also one of the most exciting aspects of the job. Don't be afraid to try new things and take risks – some of the most memorable campaigns come from bold, unconventional ideas.

As a Social Media Manager, you are the voice of the brand. Your work is highly visible. This is both a great responsibility and a remarkable opportunity. Your projects will shape the brand's public perception, build community, and drive awareness and business - take price in this!

Despite AI and automation, the human touch in social media has never been more important. Your audience wants real and honest connections, which only a human can provide. Your ability to add personality, respond with care, and tell relatable stories is what makes your brand stand out. It's this human element that builds trust, loyalty, and meaningful interactions, reminding us that behind every screen, there's a real person looking for a real connection.

Embrace continuous learning. You'll juggle platforms, stakeholders, and content ideas. The ever-changing landscape offers chances to acquire new skills and understand evolving consumer behaviors.

Some initiatives will be wildly successful, while others might not hit the mark – and that's okay. Each experience is a learning opportunity. Fail forward and embrace those mistakes as lessons.

You got this,

Anna Bertoldini
Senior Social Media Brand and Influencer Manager, NielsenIQ

Dear Social Media Manager,

Congratulations! You've got one of the best jobs available. You may ask why? Being a Social Media Manager is a diverse job in many ways.

We are Marketing Managers, Designers, and Videographers. We work in PR, customer service, and crisis management. We are therapists, problem solvers, and creative minds. We are experts not only in communication with people but also in social media. For me, this variety is what makes me excited to go to work every day.

Nonetheless, the excitement is dampened on some days because social media and people are unpredictable.

By working with social media, we work with platforms created by companies with their own agendas and goals. Sometimes, we know their agenda and can work with what we know, but more often than we would like, we don't know anything. Especially regarding the different algorithms, our knowledge is more of an educated guess, which led me to be frustrated at the beginning of my career as a Social Media Manager. You never know if your ideas that are successful today will be successful next time. But it also allows you to get creative and learn more every day.

Another reason why we never know what we get is because we work with people on the internet. People tend to take their emotions online, which can turn a good workday into a very exhausting workday on social media. Still, studies show that only 10 % of internet users comment regularly on posts or articles. That's good news for a lousy workday, so don't despair. Remember that all the work you do is not only for the people commenting, but even more so for the silent majority. You have the power to build a safe space for all the people who "only" watch your content, but do not write a comment. And this is one of the best ways to represent your company and leave a lasting good impression.

These are the four rules I live by. And maybe they'll help you too:

1. Stay curious! A change in the algorithm may be frustrating at first, but it allows you to learn something new and find a creative way to make it work for your company.

2. Be human! You are at work and have to be professional, but that doesn't mean you cannot be approachable in your DMs or comment section.

3. This, too, shall pass! The worst performance or shitstorm is just temporary. As my boss always says, we are not doing open heart surgery. No one is going to die if we make a mistake. Social media and people can be a challenge. Your best is good enough.

4. You are not alone! Being a Social Media Manager makes you part of an amazing community of people who not only know your struggles but are also willing to help you.

I wish you all the best, and stay curious.

Anna Wamsler
Social Media Manager at Mitteldeutscher Rundfunk

Dear Social Media Manager,

First, take a deep breath. You're doing a great job. If at any point you feel overwhelmed or misunderstood, re-read this letter and focus on what's important.

You're probably being pulled in all sorts of directions right now – by sales, marketing, PR, and maybe even the CEO. Each has their own priorities, and social media ends up being the place where these priorities clash. It can become confusing, but remember the most crucial thing: understand your brand's identity, tone, and strengths. That's the foundation that'll help you create content that builds genuine relationships with your audience.

What I've learned from leading social media for brands like JUST EAT and Pret is that there's more than one way to win at social media. JUST EAT's playful approach was different from Pret's focus on quality and authenticity. Yet, both strategies worked because they were true to the brands' identities.

Here are a few key points to keep in mind:

1. **Embrace Your Brand's Unique Voice:** Whether your brand is quirky, serious, or somewhere in between, let its personality shine through. Authenticity resonates with audiences far more than generic content.
2. **Focus on Building Relationships:** Social media is not just a broadcasting tool; it's a platform for two-way communication. Engage with your audience, respond to their comments, and show them that you value their input.
3. **Find the Point Between Quality and Quantity:** Find the balance between posting frequently to stay relevant and maintaining high-quality content. A few great posts are more impactful than numerous mediocre ones.

4. **Adapt and Evolve:** Social media trends change rapidly. Stay informed, be flexible, and don't be afraid to try new things. What works today might not work tomorrow, and that's okay.
5. **Take Care of Yourself:** The demands of managing social media can be intense. Make sure to balance your work with self-care to avoid burnout. Remember, a healthy, happy you is essential for your creative and professional success.

Lastly, know that it's okay to make mistakes. Every misstep is an opportunity to learn and grow. Keep experimenting, keep engaging, and most importantly, keep being you. Your authenticity is your greatest asset.

You got this!

Anthony Leung
Founder of Mean Write Hook

Dear Social Media Manager,

My business came about because I needed to create a location-independent business, and when I moved from an employed marketing lead at a charity to a business owner, I realised there was a lot to learn!

The key thing about being a Social Media Manager for me was keeping up with just how dynamic the field is. Algorithms constantly shift, trends come and go, and what worked yesterday might flop tomorrow. It's a marathon, not a sprint, so it's absolutely vital to be a lifelong learner.

One thing I wish I had known from the start is the power of repurposing content. In my work with adventure travel businesses, I've discovered that evergreen content can get a second life on platforms like Pinterest. This strategy not only saves time but also maximises the reach and impact of each piece of content. Pinterest is perfect for showcasing stunning travel photos, inspirational travel itineraries, and engaging blog posts. By understanding how to use the platform and keeping on top of all the changes it has made in the last few years, I've helped clients increase their visibility and attract new leads by adding Pinterest to their digital marketing strategy.

I have found that balancing creativity with data-driven decisions is crucial. While it's important to innovate and try new things, backing up your ideas with solid metrics and analytics is key. Knowing your audience and tailoring your content to their preferences can make all the difference in whether a piece of content is a roaring success or a total flop!

Despite the challenges, working in social media is incredibly rewarding. I love the creativity it demands, the constant learning, and the opportunity to connect with people all over the world. Inspiring and influencing through content is powerful, and it's exciting to be part of something so integral to modern communication.

For those just starting out, stay curious, be adaptable, and don't be afraid of making mistakes. Every campaign is a learning opportunity; whether it succeeds or fails, you'll go away with new ideas.

Best regards,

Carolyn Campbell-Baldwin
Director at Fresh Pin Marketing

Dear Social Media Manager,

You often hear social media managers talking about how they 'fell' into the role without ever meaning to work in social. I, dear reader, am one of those very people.

When I was a teenager, social media was just starting to creep into everyday life. And although I enjoyed organising my MySpace profile and writing Facebook statuses, I didn't ever think you could make a career out of it.

Then came my first job after university, as a Marketing Assistant responsible for writing agendas, taking minutes, and generally doing those admin tasks that no one else wants to take on. But six weeks into my role, the team's Social Media Manager left... and I was given an opportunity.

As the youngest person in the team, I was asked to start managing the university's social media channels, which at the time had an audience of over 100,000 combined. After the initial fear of hitting 'post' on those first few pieces of content subsided, I was hooked!

If I could travel back in time and speak to my 21-year-old self, with the knowledge I have now over a decade later, this is what I wish I could say:

1. Social media is a wild, ever-changing industry with new trends, updates and challenges every single day. Sometimes you'll feel like you know nothing, and sometimes you'll feel like you know everything. That's okay. Just keep learning.
2. You will win on social media when you truly, deeply, completely understand the audience you're speaking to. Know them inside and out, like they're your best friend, and you'll be able to create brilliant content. Look into

       'audience psychographics' and 'behavioural science'.
3. Social media is criminally undervalued by so many brands and business owners. Don't take it personally. A huge part of your job is to fly the flag for the power of social media as the number one way to get attention in your marketing strategy (I'm biassed, but it's true).

Lastly, have fun; you've got a very cool job. When it's feeling too intense, lock your phone away and go for a walk outside. And speak to each other - there's such a supportive community of other Social Media Managers on LinkedIn.

Happy scrolling,

Corrie Jones
Head of Social Media at StrategiQ

Dear Social Media Manager,

Breath.

Whatever might be happening in your brand's comments or DMs, it's ok. We've all been there.

The drama because no one can log in to your app, the website's crashed, or the virtual queue is causing problems. None of it is your fault of course, but it is now your responsibility.

You take it seriously, and personally.

You, the anonymous admin – fending off the hordes of keyboard warriors like some mythical hero in a fearless last stand against the forces of darkness.

Protecting the rest of your business as you sacrifice yourself for the 'greater good' at the altar of brand reputation. Repeatedly, without an end in sight.

Groundhog Day meets Lord of the Rings meets The Social Network.

Except it's much more dramatic…

You meet these challenges head on, the voice of the brand, talking directly to your customers to explain, assist and reassure. Very rarely receiving praise or thanks.

But that's ok – you carry on. We all do.

Despite these challenges you wouldn't change any of it. You see instantly when an idea starts to take off – an addictive sense of achievement you want again and again.

Creative kings and queens keeping your fingers on the pulse of culture, sport, politics, and anything else that might be relevant to your audience. Likes, comments and shares flying in – the reward for your hours of research and internet existence.

There's nothing like it in marketing. There's nothing like it in business either.

Same time tomorrow?

Dave Endsor
Senior Digital Marketing Manager (Social Media and Content Lead) at Blue Light Card

Dear Social Media Manager,

Your role offers an incredible opportunity to unleash your creativity while boosting brand awareness for businesses. One tip you might not yet know is that Emojipedia will become your best friend.

Here's my best advice: never undervalue yourself. Always define clear deliverables for your clients and be specific about your social media packages. Remember, your time is valuable, and you are an expert! Do not sell yourself short!

Here are 5 tips for you: AI can be a helpful tool, but it shouldn't be your only solution, treat your own social media presence as if it were your highest-paying client, research and create a strategy before creating content, seek mentorship, limit your screen time for certain hours to mitigate burn-out!

Being a Social Media Manager is fantastic because it allows you to constantly learn and evolve in a dynamic field. There is a rich network of professionals you can learn from and collaborate with. Don't hesitate to ask questions or seek a mentor who is further along in their career. They can provide insights and guidance, helping you avoid the pitfalls they've experienced.

Always strive to learn, hone your skills, and maintain transparency with yourself and your clients. Most importantly, stay true to yourself!

Diana Rapine
Owner *of* Palm + Pine Marketing and Design

"Remember, your time is valuable, and you are an expert! Do not sell yourself short!"

Dear Social Media Manager,

Social media isn't easy – it's going to take over your life, so make sure you love it before you dedicate yourself to this career.

It's a tough hustle, where you have to keep up with the development and constant changes, updates and U-turns of the platforms and their policies, and client requirements on the other side.

This being said… it can also be incredibly rewarding. When you see a piece of content you worked so hard on take-off, bring people joy, make them happy, or just see people find what you worked on informative and useful. At the end of the whole chain – your client satisfied with your work and feeling they made the right choice by working with you, over anyone else in the business.

Facebook might have long moved from their mantra of earlier days – I was there, I remember – "Move fast, break things" – but I would say it still rings true for a lot of social media. There's no one-size-fits-all recipe or a formula for success. It's a lot about trial and error, figuring things out and then getting the most out of the results of your own research, that works with the tone of voice, the audience you have, and the brand. What works for one brand, isn't necessarily going to work for the other.

Quite likely, it actually won't.

Don't copy – try to be original. Look up to others for inspiration but always try and put your own angle and touch on your work, so it fits the ecosystem you're in – as no two ecosystems are the same. Even the same brand, in two local markets, might have to communicate in different ways, because of the differences in cultural sensibilities.

The industry is great – but it's also very unforgiving. Very often you're only seen as good as your last project was. Don't let it get to you, however, and always remember your own worth. If you get knocked down, get up and don't let them keep you down (thanks, Chumbawamba – you got me through more than you could even imagine). There will be times when you're on top of the world, and there will be times when you'll feel you're fighting against the whole force of the universe, made of demanding clients or employers, budget restrictions and algorithms working against you. That's just what it is, however there's always ways to carve out a niche and do something amazing, which is what gives that sweet taste of victory we all chase and you'll be getting that, too.

No matter how tough it is at any given moment, just keep going – brighter times are always ahead, this whole industry is a sinewave and as long as you keep on making moves, you'll come out victorious. I've been through that more times than I can count, and I know I will again, and again, and again. Don't focus on hardships. Focus on the victories that are around the corner. Always.

Dynamitri Joachim Nawrot
Social Media Manager

Dear Social Media Manager,

Believe it or not, there was a time where being a Social Media Manager was completely underappreciated. And granted, we're not quite over the hurdle of everyone *thinking* they know how to do what we do, but we are getting somewhere with the role becoming increasingly recognised as one for exuberant talent and creativity. Even after over a decade in the industry, I'm still learning, still growing, and at times still doubting. I still spend a large part of my days trapped in the clutches of impostor syndrome, but the thrill of seeing a social strategy through to the end never <u>ever</u> gets dull.

I wish someone had told me when I started out to not be afraid of failing. The biggest enemy to creativity is self-doubt, and I found myself holding back so much more in my twenties. So many social media concepts that never quite made it off the cutting room floor, could have maybe flourished if only they saw the light of day. I often think about concepts I designed for brands that never passed through legal, or strategies I hope I'll find a home for one day, but if you have the opportunity to test the crazy idea, then make sure you test the crazy idea! Some of those concepts you swear blind will skyrocket may fail, and something you put together in half an hour on Canva might excel, but ideas deserve to be tested as that is ultimately how you learn and grow.

Another important thing to remember is things change all the time. The algorithms, the latest "hacks," trends, and platform features and whilst it's important to keep up to date with what's going on, honestly it's impossible to be an expert at it all. Find something you love, and are good at, and hone in on that skill. Whether that's a platform that you love spending time on, or a particular industry that fills your cup. You may fall in love with industries you never thought you'd know (I once worked with a dust extraction company and LOVED it).

With the rise of AI and new generations changing the way we consume content, it's truly hard to predict how the social media landscape will transform. However, consumers are more social media savvy than ever before. They want to know what a brand is about, and they use social media to connect with the real people behind the social accounts. This paves the way for businesses to use communities and people-first content, and presents unique opportunities for Social Media Managers to rewrite a brand's story.

This industry can, at times, be full of people trying to tell you how to be, what to act like, and what to create. But it's so important to carve your own path, and try to have fun as much as possible. Your content will flourish if you love what you do.

Emma Glover
Founder of Social Media Agency, Victress.

Dear Social Media Manager,

It's Fab here, your new marketing BFF - and professional hype girl.

Before we even begin, I want to tell you that you're doing great. I want you to read that again. You are doing great. You're doing a fantastic job, and what a hell of a job you're doing. Let that sink in before you continue reading this letter.

I started working in social media as my first job in marketing. Calling it a job is probably not as accurate, as I was doing this on the side while studying at university.

I managed social media for record labels and PR agencies in the music industry.

But then, eventually, I landed my first full-time marketing job as a Community Manager for a ticketing company in London. I realised I had a whole new playground to tap into, as social media was still relatively new for brands and businesses.

One thing I wish I knew back then is that being a Social Media Manager is not just about creating content. It's about being a connector, a mediator between brands and customers.

I wish I knew the pitfalls it would bring and the stresses of being the person who has to be the messenger of both wins and complaints.

Remember, what you're doing is not just creating posts on Canva or responding to comments. You're building relationships, and your work is essential in creating better marketing strategies and foundations.
Now, with over 15 years in the marketing industry, I want to stress the importance of taking care of yourself, your mental health, and

your energy. This is so important not just for your personal well-being, but also for the quality and enjoyment of your work. It will impact the relationships you build online and the energy you bring to the space.

Social Media Managers are incredible networkers, often without realising it. So, my advice is to reframe the way you see your role—as a relationship builder. Take breaks when needed, not just for screen time but to refill your cup and enjoy the quiet in a noisy online world.

As a connector and networker, you witness the amazing work, effort, and results your brand, company, or clients bring into the world.

You get to be a cheerleader for yourself and others, and you're part of a fantastic community—the Social Media Managers community is pretty awesome!

So, as a sign-off, I'll say it one more time: you're doing great. I mean it. I'm proud of you, and you should be too. As your favourite hype girl, I'm always here to cheer you on

Fab Giovanetti
CEO of Alt Marketing School

Dear Social Media Manager,

After 13 years in the digital marketing industry, here is the advice I would offer:

You don't have to do it all. Having a niche is okay and, in the long run, better for you. There are many social media roles out there that expect you to do everything, but don't burn yourself out.

Say yes to opportunities and figure the rest out later. If you're worried a role, you're applying for is too challenging, go for it anyway. The worst outcome is they say no and you learn something.

Don't be afraid to ask for more money when you're being offered a position. Too many people in our industry charge too little for their hard work. Look at the amount of revenue you're bringing in and compare it to industry averages—do your homework.

Learn how to make paid ads, even if you don't want to be a paid ads specialist. Knowing and understanding this part of marketing is important.

Learn from the people you work with, both on your team and on other teams. Understand the basics of what happens outside your department. This will give you a deeper understanding of the business ecosystem, so you can do your job better and be a great teammate.

Create something—it doesn't matter what—and post your creations online. Not only can you test marketing hypotheses by posting your own work, but having a creative outlet improves your mental health and your actual work while building a portfolio.

Collaborate. It's not only a great way to network, but you can learn a lot from working with other people both in and outside of your industry.

Remember to take breaks from social media and mind your mental health. In this industry, we spend a lot of time online. Offline time is necessary, so make sure to take care of yourself.

Best wishes,
Grace Clemens
CEO & Founder of SGC Marketing

Dear Social Media Manager,

For those of you just starting out in social media, let this be your sign you chose right! I hope you fall in love with the future possibilities this career can offer you and walk away with something to bring into your daily grind. For you seasoned vets, I hope this letter leaves you with a spark of inspiration and a reminder of how cool our jobs really are!

Reflecting on the past decade in the 'adult world,' working a 'big girl job,' I feel incredibly blessed to have experienced the journey this career has offered me. Accepting my first role as a Social Media Coordinator in San Diego has given me some of my best friends and best memories. From sailing around Croatia on a yacht to watching Pipeline going off in the winter, and throwing a 1,000+ person mini-music festival, my social media career has been nothing short of epic. Here are some of the lessons I've learned along the way ...

A little bit extra goes a long way.
Show up a little early. Stay a bit late. Raise your hand to help out. Make genuine connections. Respond to that comment. Send some product to a dedicated follower. Write a handwritten note. These small actions can lead you to amazing experiences, connections and opportunities. Your special touch to projects won't go unnoticed - by coworkers, peers, and customers!

Take the time to brand yourself.
While we may not feel like creating for ourselves after creating and posting all day for someone else, it's essential to! Take the time to invest in yourself and make it *fun!* Dedicating time to build your personal brand will keep you at the forefront of content creation, differentiate you from the competition, increase your visibility, and establish you as a credible professional. This job is temporary, your personal brand is not.

Social is what YOU make it to be.
Whether you're into analytics and growth plans, feeling inspired to get creative, or looking to engage with customers, social media allows you to design your job. Dive into the data, unleash your creativity, or become the bridge between the brand and its audience. The possibilities are endless, and it's up to you to carve your own path.

When people say 'anyone can do that,' remember, you're THE hub for the brand.

You are the gateway for new consumers and the anchor for core supporters. You are the mouthpiece for all things happening within the brand. You need to be plugged into product launches, partnerships, creative execution, customer service, and any other crucial moment! All while staying on trend and up to date on your platforms. Remember—you are indispensable.

Embrace the journey, stay passionate, and continue making your mark in the world of social media.

-G

Grace McLaughlin
Brand Community Director at Blenders Eyewear

Dear Social Media Manager

No two days are the same, right? Every day, we learn something new, because there isn't another industry that changes as rapidly as digital marketing. We talk about reach, engagement, algorithms, and return on investment – and then try to figure them all out for our clients.

Marketing itself has never changed – the theories are the same; and the concepts apply to any business.

But what *has* changed is how we deliver the messages to our audience. Traditional marketing still exists and social media is still comparatively new (and, if you were born in this century, you don't know a life before it). It just means we now have quicker access to market, and a much more quantifiable method – we no longer rely on monthly readership figures for our local newspaper or quarterly listener statistics for our local radio.

John Wanamaker once famously complained, "half the money I spend on advertising is wasted, and the trouble is I don't know which half."

Now, we now have a wealth of knowledge and experience at our fingertips. We have smart phones and tablets full of social media apps – and we use these apps to quantify our outputs. These apps help us to much more agile and deliver quick, real-time information. We can change between platforms, using different methods such as Facebook groups or Instagram Reels or LinkedIn newsletters or TikTok Shop.

Arguably, social media has become one of the biggest cornerstones of the marketing mix.

And while us Social Media Managers find it hard to keep on top of it all, it also keeps us alive – we thrive on finding the latest feature, the best advice, the algorithmic boosts – all to make sure that we (and our clients) are staying at the forefront of the audience's mind. One of the best things about being a Social Media Manager is seeing the positive change you can make to someone's business, their income and, ultimately, their lifestyle.

My advice is to lead from the front – manage your own social media like you would that of a client. Get your own strategy in place; work out your niche; find your ideal clients; and get into a rhythm of consistency. After all, practice makes perfect. And the niche is important because our clients expect us to be everything, but it's better for them (and us) to know what we are good at.

And throughout it all, always be *intentionally* yourself. Your clients buy into you. Steven Bartlett may have had a social media agency worth hundreds of millions, but his clients like him. Why? Because he's always himself.

One of the biggest challenges is that there are more bad guys than good, because the entry point is so low – anybody with a phone and a couple of apps can claim to be a Social Media Manager. This is why we shouldn't just sell our services – we sell the vision, dream and end goal – i.e. what can we achieve for our clients that others can't. This is why we should never look around us – don't worry about competitors. Find your niche, always be yourself, and trust in your abilities. And finally, don't tell people how good you are – show them.

Stay awesome, my friends.
With love

Gus Bhandal
Founder of The M Guru: Digital Marketing Agency

Dear Social Media Manager,

Isn't it crazy to think even just a decade ago many of our jobs wouldn't even exist or would be encompassed by other roles?

While you still see skin-crawling terms like 'Social Media Guru' thrown around, it's extraordinary to see how far businesses have come to take social media seriously as a part of their marketing strategy. Social media holds so much weight these days.

I am sure that I am not the only one who found my career path in social media seemingly by chance, in the sense that that wasn't what I was actively seeking out.

What I wish I knew about the social media industry before joining it, is simply knowing that it existed in a professional sense and could become a viable career. I've always been a creative person who loves to express myself through writing and visuals, and for that reason, I studied journalism at university, but I quickly realised this wouldn't be the environment for me. I never even considered there'd be other avenues such as marketing. I discovered marketing shortly after finishing my degree through further career research and an internship, and that's when everything just felt like it clicked into place. It ticked the boxes of what I was interested in and looking for. At this time, I started working with social media and the rest is history.

My top tips when it comes to social media are firstly to just be human, even as a brand. People want to hear from people, not from a robot, so have some fun. That doesn't necessarily mean you have to go all out silly, but injecting personality into your content can make a huge difference and makes the finished result more engaging. Lean into your brand's mission and tone of voice to craft a bespoke personality that makes sense for you.

Secondly, don't be afraid to try something new on social media.

It is easy to fall into habits or your comfort zone and avoid changing up your content. However, testing new approaches can keep your output fresh and provide insights on what does or doesn't work for your brand's presence. It is also okay if the test doesn't go well or the content type performs poorly, all results tell you something and can help steer you in the right direction to what does work for you.

I love and enjoy how dynamic social media is and how it facilitates creativity. No two days are the same and there is always a new format, trend or content type that is on the horizon. It offers endless opportunities, and let's be honest, it's just plain old fun to work with!

Holly Hammond
Social Media Coordinator at Technology Networks

Dear Social Media Manager,

I have worked in social media for the best part of twenty years (which makes me really old). My one bit of advice would be this; in order to best embrace and prepare for the future it is worth understanding the past. Before you future gaze and comprehend the 'now' – gain insights from looking backwards.

1) Commerce

An understanding of the key value proposition of each social media platform will put you at an advantage over other social media managers.

Friends Reunited was the first social network to be popular in the UK and launched in 2000 and was sold to ITV in 2005 for £175million. It was an early example of a subscription model. TikTok has always excelled at being an entertainment destination but increasingly sees itself as a retail destination with its TikTok shop.

Social media managers can map user journeys that reflect the commercial considerations of the platforms they are native to.

2) Culture

Vine, the 15 second video app that was eventually swallowed up by X (formerly Twitter) had a unique culture, unique memes and a way of behaviour that was seen and used by content creators used in the early days of TikTok. LinkedIn was centred around jobs and professional networking but has morphed towards thought leadership, work place culture and personal branding. It is further morphing towards video content.

By looking at how audiences on each platform behave, Social Media Managers can predict how culture and behaviour will change going forward.

3) Communities

TikTok started life devoted to music and dance content. What new platforms that are currently super serving one niche interest or community, have the ability to broaden their remit to serve multiple communities? In the peak of MySpace, around 2005 to 2008, it revolutionised audience relationships with emerging music acts and had incredible relationships with music rights holders, foreshadowing TikTok's relationships with music labels now.

So, in short, look backwards a bit and reflect on what has happened before, in order to educate yourself about what is happening now and what might happen in the future.

Yours Sincerely
James Erskine
CEO of Rocket

Dear Social Media Manager,

One of the biggest realisations I've had is that social media is all about community building. It's not about chasing likes or creating the most aesthetically pleasing content. It's about crafting content that truly connects with people, providing a platform for voices to be heard, and creating spaces where people feel they belong.

Understanding this has completely changed how I approach social media. It's not just a content creation job—it's a strategic role that impacts both culture and business. Here are a few tips and pieces of advice that I think can help make your journey as a social media manager a bit smoother:

1. **Set Boundaries**: Remember, you are not the accounts you manage. The world won't end if you're not online 24/7. Find a job and a manager who respect and understand this boundary. Your well-being is crucial for sustaining your creativity and effectiveness.

2. **Focus on Community**: Our role as social media managers is to build and nurture communities. It's not about going viral; it's about creating lasting connections and fostering a sense of belonging among your audience.

3. **Balance Creativity and Strategy**: Enjoy the creative aspects of your role, but always align your creativity with strategic business goals. The magic happens at the intersection of creativity and strategy, where you can drive real impact.

4. **Educate and Advocate**: Many still don't fully grasp the value of social media. Take every chance you get to educate others about its importance in building a community that cares about your brand. Investing in social media is essentially investing in a loyal and engaged

community.

I feel incredibly fortunate to be in a position where I can champion the role of Social Media Managers as community builders. We're at a point where social media is leading the marketing mix, and I'm excited about what the future holds.
The Social Media Managers of today are the CMOs of tomorrow, and we're shaping the future of marketing together.

Working in social media allows us to have a meaningful impact on building communities, leveraging creativity, and driving business goals through cultural relevance. While there are challenges—such as the need for broader recognition of social media's value—these are opportunities for us to advocate for and elevate our profession.

Remember, we are in the business of building communities. Carpe Diem!

Best,

Joe Teo
CEO of HeyOrca

Dear Social Media Manager,

The world of social media is an exciting, diverse, and fun place. It's also hectic and always changing. Once you dodge the trolls and politics, you'll begin to see the beauty of the endless creativity and connection social has to offer. Having been in and around social for 15 years, I've learned a lot of valuable lessons. If I could travel back in time and offer advice to my younger self navigating the ever-evolving world of social media, here's what I'd say:

First, always be curious! This industry thrives on it. Stay on top of trends, examine those campaigns, and dig into the "why" behind what works. Curiosity will fuel creativity and it will propel you to stay ahead of the curve.

Next, never stop learning! Social media is practically a living organism, constantly morphing and adapting. Be a lifelong learner. Just as you need to embrace curiosity, you need to be willing and open to constant learning. Over-consume industry publications and insights, go to conferences, and network with other professionals. The knowledge you gain and the people you meet might be the key to unlocking success later down the road.

Don't be afraid to fail. Test, try and tinker. As these platforms evolve, so should your approach. You need to experiment with different content formats, test out features, and take calculated risks. It'll pay off, but you have to step outside your comfort zone.

Finally, roll with the punches. Buckle up, because change is the only constant in social media. Algorithms shift, platforms update, and trends fade. Others may not understand your role or the value you bring. They may even disregard your expertise, but it's all part of the path you're on. You'll face challenges everywhere you look, but as long as you develop resilience and the ability to adapt on a dime you will succeed. Embrace the unexpected, and see challenges as opportunities to learn and refine your approach.

This industry is a whirlwind, but it's also incredibly rewarding. Trust your gut and your expertise. Remember, your curiosity, willingness to learn, and ability to adapt will be your super powers. So, stay curious, keep learning, experiment relentlessly, and most importantly, have fun!

Sincerely,

Jonathan Hatch
Global Talent Brand Manager at Zoom

Dear Social Media Manager,

I see you.

The overworking. The "Oh your jobs so easy- I wish I could just scroll on Instagram all day." The scrambling to post reactive content from the most unconventional environments. The new industry trend and platform updates every week. The repeated question, "So... what is it you actually do?" from older relatives who can't quite grasp what social media is. The overwhelm. The internal eyeroll you make when your client or boss thinks you can click your fingers and magically make a post go viral. The bloody algorithm changes. The endless attacks on social media managers: "That's not even a real job." The lack of work-life balance. The pressure. The inability to take your own social media detox. The battles with measuring and explaining ROI...

You're not alone.

On the days you feel like you're drowning and can't quite keep your head above water, reverse the script on that painstaking list I've just written and remember this:

Your job is pretty damn cool. It's fun, it's innovative and you're a lifelong learner.

Yes, you might sometimes have to juggle 17 plates. And yes, one or two may smash from time to time. But next time 'round, you'll learn from your mistakes. Plus, you must already thrive off chaos (even a little) to have chosen this career path...

If you're as passionate about marketing as I am, I'm sure you'll agree that as demanding as it is, there's no role quite like being a Social Media Manager.

It allows you to build connections and bring people together. You can create, nurture and strengthen communities. Make a genuine difference. Captivate through storytelling. Express yourself creatively. Learn a diverse range of stills. Wear many hats (who else can say they're a strategist, photographer, copywriter, graphic designer, analyst AND community manager!?) You learn to make better data-driven decisions. Seeing an idea come to life in a campaign, exactly how you envisioned it in your mind. Being hyper-aware of your surroundings because there's inspiration everywhere. When you finally create *that* viral post. Exceeding your targets and making everyone happy. Solving people's problems and alleviating pain points. Getting to collaborate with creative geniuses. Knowing you have limitless potential.

Yup, it might be fast-paced and cut-throat, and it's certainly not for the faint of heart. But you get the opportunities to create and shape the messages people see every day.

Knowing you can make that kind of impact makes it all worth it.

Karla McNeilage
Social Media Marketer & Copywriter
Founder of Wave Socials

Dear Social Media Manager,

If you asked me 10 years ago if I'd be working in social media, I'd have no clue what you were talking about.
As a Journalism major, I had envisioned working at a print magazine in New York City as an editor. I watched too many romantic comedies growing up.

Once I reached my third year of undergrad, I began internships at local publications. I thoroughly enjoyed writing and storytelling. However, by my final year of undergrad, it was time to start submitting job applications. This was rigorous, grueling, and emotionally draining. With rejection after rejection, I watched as my dream of working at a magazine was slowly slipping away before my eyes. Just as I was feeling my self-esteem hit subterranean levels, I saw a job posting that read, "Marketing Manager".

Now, eight years later, I am deeply engulfed in the world of social media at a global life science company, and I love every minute of it.

One of my favorite aspects of the job is that I don't have to give up my creative drive. Those same journalism characteristics of writing and storytelling are strongly evident in the social media space. Working cross-collaboratively with creative teams and marketing stakeholders, I'm able to express myself and exercise that creative side of my brain.

Social media is multi-faceted – it is not one singular thing. Whatever you are interested in, whatever your especially skilled in, you can focus on in a social media career. Are you exceptionally skilled in graphic design? Work on a creative team for social projects. Are you detail-oriented and love organizing or managing projects? You can lead a team of social media managers and head large-scale projects.

This is truly what I love about social media. It offers a multitude of opportunities with new areas and challenges popping up on nearly a daily basis.

The social media road is endless. I can't wait to see where it takes you.

Best,

Kate Berry
Social Media Manager at MilliporeSigma

Dear Social Media Manager,

Sometimes a post that you've worked one for hours will flop. Sometimes a video you posted on a whim will go viral. It happens.

But bestie, it's just not that serious.

So PLEASE don't be so hard on yourself when things don't go to plan.

Algorithms change, audience preferences shift, and what works one day might not work the next. Every post, regardless of its performance, is a learning opportunity (yes I know that's hard to see when you're stuck on 200 TikTok views and trying to tell your manager why, but trust me).

When something flops, it's not a reflection of your worth or skills. It's just a chance to gather valuable insights. Look at the data. Analyse it. Was it the timing? The content? The audience targeting? Use these insights to refine your strategy.

Stay curious, stay flexible, and most importantly, stay kind to yourself. Your creativity and dedication are what drive your success. Keep learning, keep growing, and trust the process. Finally, don't let anyone dull your sparkle.

You don't *need* to mimic others or conform to stand out.
Your unique personality, quirks, and perspectives are what make you memorable.

So be yourself, you're fab!
Xoxo

Katie Murphy
Head of Social Media at Early Years Resources

"When something flops, it's not a reflection of your worth or skills. It's just a chance to gather valuable insights."

Dear Social Media Manager,

Welcome to the wild, wonderful, and sometimes wacky world of social media management! Whether you're just starting or have been in the trenches for years, there's always something new to learn and enjoy about this ever-evolving industry.
When I started this digital journey 15+ years ago, I wish someone had told me a few key things. So here are my pearls of wisdom, sprinkled with a bit of humour and heart.

The Learning Never Stops
You might think you know everything about Facebook's algorithm or Instagram's latest features, but trust me, it changes faster than you can say "trending hashtag." Continuous learning isn't just a nice-to-have—it's a must. Join industry groups, take part in webinars, and never stop asking questions. Passion fuels purpose, and staying curious keeps you at the top of your game.

Work-life Balance is a Myth (Sort Of)
Let's be real—managing a brand's social media presence can feel like a 24/7 job. Notifications at all hours, crises that seem to pop up only on weekends, and the pressure to always be "on" can be overwhelming. My advice? Set boundaries early. It's okay to mute notifications after hours and take a break. Your mental health is just as important as that next viral (yes, that beautiful word we all love) post. Gulp.

The Rollercoaster of Metrics
One day, your post will break engagement records. Next, it's crickets. Don't let the numbers define your worth. Understand the analytics, sure, but remember: behind every like, share, and comment is a human being. Focus on creating meaningful connections, and the metrics will follow.

Collaboration is Key
No social media manager is an island. Collaborate with your team,

bounce ideas off each other, and don't hesitate to ask for help. Some of my best campaigns were born from brainstorming sessions over coffee (one perfect cup a day does the trick). A little sarcastic banter never hurts!

Embrace the Fun
Despite the challenges, there's so much joy in what we do. From the thrill of a successful campaign to the satisfaction of a well-crafted post, find the fun in your work. Celebrate the wins, laugh off the fails, and always keep your enthusiasm alive.

Social media is more than just a job—it's a journey. Enjoy the ride, stay curious, and remember: you've got this.

Cheers to your success,

Kim "Kimpossible" Stavropoulos
Consulting Digital Marketer, Social Media Strategist, and Copywriter.

P.S. Always make friends with the design team

Dear Social Media Manager,

I have great pride in telling others that I work in Social Media Marketing, as this is a role that I didn't even know existed until 6 years ago, and what a wicked job it is. Normally the first thing I'm asked after telling people what I do is, "do you scroll on Facebook all day?". Well, you best believe I have the script for the answer now, but I also love educating people on what I do for a living.

So, let's get into it!

I fell in love with social media when I joined StrategiQ Marketing Agency as a Marketing Executive. I started with two clients (who I still work with to this day) and if I were to look back now on some of the posts I created back then, I would probably cringe, but it is also an indication of how far I have grown in such a short amount of time.

Working agency-side means I do everything that social media marketing entails, from content creation and influencer marketing to community management and video creation. You name it, I do it. But this has given me a chance to learn my strengths and weaknesses within my role, which means I can lean on those around me for support, if need be, whilst also sharing my expertise in certain areas.

Organic social media is one of the most demanding, yet most rewarding jobs. You can often find the sweet spot of what works for your client, but the challenge is to keep that flow going. If you can crack the code of understanding your audience, you're halfway there. You need to make sure you do that initial research before you even undertake your strategy because if not, you will be talking to the wrong people and not see the return you want for your hard work.

If I leave you with one bit of advice if you want to get into the social media marketing world, is to go with the flow when it comes to platform changes, algorithm updates and trends. Make sure you're ready to adapt at any given moment because if you allow yourself to be flexible, you will give your business, accounts and content the best chance to thrive, so you ensure you don't get left behind.

Lauren Grubb
Social Media Executive at StrategiQ

Dear Social Media Manager,

As I celebrate my 15th anniversary in the B2B social media industry this year (hard to believe, I know), I wanted to share with you the key insight that has transformed my approach to social media strategy: realising that the majority of your B2B audience isn't ready to buy your product or service right now, no matter what growth or demand generation theories suggest.

Research from marketing scientists such as the Ehrenberg-Bass Institute shows that about 95% of your potential buyers aren't in a position to purchase. They might not even be aware they have a problem your product solves. The real purpose of your social channels, from organic posts to paid ads, from employee advocacy to social selling—isn't lead generation. It's about getting in front of your audience and building a relationship so that when they are ready to buy, whether in months or years, you're their top choice.

Fellow social pro, the good news is that social media is the perfect tool to build the brand awareness and communities needed to earn your audience's demand when the time comes. Focus on understanding your audience: who they are, what they care about and how you can connect with them beyond just selling a product. Identify the problems you can solve for them, leveraging multiple B2B social touchpoints—from organic content to influencer partnerships, repeatedly engage and build those long-term relationships.

Community building takes time. And while direct response activities like webinars have their place on B2B social, shifting from trying to generate immediate demand to building trust and value has been a game-changer for me.

Lena Weber-Reed
Global Social Media Lead at GMS

"It's about getting in front of your audience and building a relationship so that when they are ready to buy, whether in months or years, you're their top choice."

Dear Social Media Manager,

I hope you are enjoying your time reading all these letters. It must feel like a lot. I know my first few years in the social media landscape were very overwhelming learning tips, researching trends and trying to stay up to date with the ever-changing algorithm (before you ask, I couldn't. Nobody manages to stay up to date with it). So, I want to share the most important lesson of my social media years.

I once worked for a start-up where the founder was friends with a very well-known makeup brand. They would meet every fortnight to chat and share business tips, which in principle sounds great but this often resulted in her asking us to imitate what they were doing. If it works for them, it should work for us, right? Unsurprisingly, it didn't. Not only because we were a team of 4 and they were 20, but also because the style of content that worked for them, didn't resonate with our audience. We were being pulled in a thousand directions copying other brands when we should have used that time to learn what our followers wanted.

There's a lot of comparison in the social media world. People will tell you that posting at 6 am on a Tuesday will increase your engagement, that reels are key to breaking Instagram, that you should add CTAs to every LinkedIn post in the comments and many more. While this probably works for some, don't be discouraged if it doesn't work for you.

Social media is not a one-size-fits-all. Don't go crazy imitating other brands' strategies or successes. Instead, use your own metrics to dictate what works for you and your audience. Breathe in, test, optimise and keep improving!

Magali Mas D'Amato
Marketing Consultant at Nationwide

"Social media is not a one-size-fits-all."

Dear Social Media Manager,

Can you describe social media in one word? Just one.

Impossible.

And you want to start a career in social media?

Welcome to the exciting world of creative campaigns, brand storytelling, and... well, it's not always sunshine and rainbows.

Starting a career in social media can be exciting, but it also comes with surprises. Surprises no one warned you about.
I was once in your shoes, clueless and overwhelmed by all the options. But guess what?

I have figured it out and now I want to share 3 tips I wish I'd known before I started my career in social media.

1. Start building your own experience

We've all seen entry-level roles asking for 2-3 years of experience and it makes my head spin. Building a strong foundation in social media doesn't always require a traditional job. Start offering your services to local businesses, volunteer for non-profit organisations or undertake personal projects. You can do it!

2. Clients are everywhere

Finding your first client can be daunting, I know. But networking is your secret weapon! Attend industry events, join online communities and leverage platforms like LinkedIn to connect with professionals. Don't underestimate the power of a genuine conversation – it could lead to your next big opportunity!

3. Don't trust everything you see about social media

What do you mean I won't spend a whole day every day in Canva, adjusting cute photos for my client? While creativity is important, social media requires a blend of skills like data analytics, strategy, project management etc. What do you mean Maja, it's not about cool ads? Well, I have to tell you it's about understanding your audience, building relationships and delivering value.

This is just the beginning of your social media adventure. The world is full of opportunities and only if you dare, you can achieve great things and change social media for the better!

I wish you all the best on your journey.

Maja Ivić
Social Media Strategist

Dear Social Media Manager,

Buckle up, this is a wild ride. This industry is constantly changing and your day to day will never look the same. Amidst all the chaos, you will find fulfilment in your work and all the stories you're able to tell. As I am four years into my social media career working primarily in the restaurant industry, I feel like this advice can be beneficial to anyone that is either starting out in this field, or a seasoned professional that needs a fresh look at our role.

To get started, it's crucial to fully understand your brand. You want your customers to recognize your company and see its consistent presence echoed across all platforms and marketing efforts. A well-defined brand identity also guides your decisions, making it easier to choose the right platforms, partnerships, and campaigns that best represent your business. This consistency will build trust with your audience, eventually making them feel like they truly *know* you. A strong brand identity acts as a compass, ensuring all your content and interactions are aligned with your core values and mission, which further solidifies your brand's reputation.

Once you have a grasp on your brand, you can distinguish your company from competitors and lean into your strengths. In a world flooded with information and advertisements, standing out is essential. It's important to highlight your unique selling points through engaging content, interactive posts, and compelling visuals. Don't be afraid to experiment! Testing new ideas can lead to unexpected successes and insights. Learn to accept that failing isn't a setback, just an opportunity to learn.

Stay relevant! The internet evolves rapidly with constant changes in platforms, algorithms, tools and trends. Keeping up-to-date and educated on these advancements so you can have the knowledge to adapt and thrive. Personally, I subscribe to a variety of social media newsletters, I reach out to other Social Media

Managers in my network and attend webinars to stay informed.

In this role, where creativity is a constant demand, it's common to experience a 'creative block'. Trust me, I want every post to go viral and get a lot of engagement, but we all know that isn't always the case. What has helped me to get out of this rut is talking to people in other branches of my company, gathering insight from the owners that built the brand from the ground up, or engaging with the audience that buys the product. These stakeholders give me insight into many different aspects that make up this business. Can you feature them and tell their story? Or gather the knowledge they've shared with you to highlight another part of the business.

Embrace the challenges, celebrate even the small successes, and never lose sight of the powerful stories waiting to be told through your work!

Enjoy the ride,

Mandie Geller
Head of Social & Photography at Puesto, Marisi & Roma Norte

Dear Social Media Manager,

Embarking on this journey, I wish I had realized sooner that social media management was a viable career path. For 11 years, I navigated through various roles, only to find that each step inadvertently prepared me for the niche where my true passion lies. Had I recognized this path earlier, I would have dedicated myself solely to mastering the art and science of social media.

The beauty of our role is the blend of creativity and analytical rigor it demands. However, this also means facing the common misjudgement of our work as trivial—overshadowed by the lighter side of social media, such as viral cat videos and memes. Yet, it's in these platforms where the potential for global impact and real-time engagement lies, offering us unparalleled opportunities to craft influential campaigns and measure their success instantly.

Working at LabX Media Group has been a fulfilling chapter in my career. The collaboration across various departments has not only broadened my perspective but also deepened my appreciation for the intricacies of our work. It is exhilarating to be part of a larger narrative, contributing to a cohesive vision rather than competing in silos.

My best advice to anyone navigating this field is to prioritize work-life balance. Social media never sleeps, and it's easy to blur the lines between personal and professional time. Treat your online interactions as part of your portfolio; remember, a comment made in haste could be viewed by a potential employer or client. Every post, reply, or tweet should reflect the professionalism you want to project.

One of the toughest challenges we face is managing expectations. Those not immersed in the nuances of social media often underestimate the complexity involved in what may seem like simple tasks. Whether it's adapting content across multiple platforms with varying requirements or handling customer interactions—every element requires thoughtful strategy and patience.

In closing, embrace the multifaceted nature of our work. The rapid pace and constant evolution of social media demand resilience and adaptability. By sharing our experiences and insights, we pave the way for those who will one day take the reins, ensuring the continued growth and dynamism of this vibrant industry.

Sincerely,

Mandy Karl
Social Media Specialist at LabX Media Group

Dear Social Media Manager,

If I had a time machine and could go back and talk to my younger self there are four key things I would like to tell my younger self to help make my job as a Social Media Manager a bit easier.

1. Feeling Isolated at Home

When you work as a Social Media Manager, you will most likely be working for yourself at home. This can be isolating as contact will generally be via email with the occasional face-to-face call. Make sure that you do #2 and get an accountability partner or buddy and meet up regularly. Get outside every day and exercise. You'll have a dog and this will be a blessing.

2. Find Your Tribe

Building that all-important community (or tribe) is so important. That came from joining online groups, participating in training courses and going to face-to-face networking events. Even if you're not sure if it will be the group for you, try it out as you never know who may meet, or who they can introduce you to! One of these groups may turn into a membership and you'll be a founding member and get lots of benefits to help you and your business.

3. Describing What You Do to Friends and Family

Not everyone will understand what you do. You will try and describe what you do, sometimes multiple times and family and friends just won't get it.

But that's fine and you're not alone with that. Once you have your tribe you will be with people who understand and share your frustration and who can laugh with you at the silly comments you get. Such as: "You just 'play' on your phone all day!" OR "When will you get a proper job?"

The way to deal with it is to find a simple way of explaining what you do in terms that make sense. So, whether it's: "I help local small businesses shout about what they do to attract more customers, which brings more revenue for their business."

4. Trust Your Gut Instinct!
If you don't want to work with someone for whatever reason, your gut or there are red flags. Don't come up with an excuse, just say: "We're not a good fit, but I can recommend someone for you." and send them to a Social Media Manager directory. You'll be in a community that has one!

So, my younger self, make sure that you pay attention to these three pearls of wisdom, don't worry about feeling isolated, find a community and quickly draft that killer phrase that describes what you do and how you help people.

Good Luck and have fun!

Marianne Avery
LinkedIn™ Confidence Coach

Dear Social Media Manager,

Buckle up because you're in for the most unpredictable ride of your life. One day, you're soaring on the meme train, and the next, you're scrambling for 60-second video talent.

Your role is often misunderstood – currently thought of as someone who just "posts" a few pictures and calls it a day. But we, the social team, know the complex nature of your day-to-day.

You are a multiple-hat social guru. The person who is expected to be a Project Manager, Videographer, Creative Director, stay on top of every rising trend, the one person on the team meant to just "get" culture, people, and the psychological response of those on the opposite end of thumb-stopping content.

You are a strategic powerhouse driven by many numbers and metrics: ROI, ER, CPC, and whatever other acronym the social world expects from you. But you sometimes love to just flow with the vibe of social – the feeling of reading and understanding community sentiment.

You are a respected but often overlooked part of the marketing department.

And I wish I could tell you it gets easier, but you just get better. So, no matter the cliche, you truly learn to navigate the social world with grace, empower the dips in data, and truly not take things personally (because sometimes a flop is just a flop).

So, as you begin or continue to navigate your career, know that the journey is ever-changing, and it's up to you to stand out in a sea of sameness. Don't get discouraged by the 579 rounds of revisions or 968 "no's."

Because you are the expert. You sit in the trenches. And you are the one who is on the cusp of community response and reaction.

It is ok to be discouraged by the pushback. It is ok to feel like the creative might not get approved. But I promise you, through the trials and tribulations, the millions of rejected ideas, and the continual push for on-trend creative, you will find a way to break the mould and break through the
noise. You will be on the edge of creating thumb-stopping content.

Overall, great content will all come down to listening to the community and creating content that they want, rather than the content your leadership (or marketers) wants.

So, be patient. Be adaptable. Most importantly, be vigilant in creating content that resonates with your audience and not everyone else's.

May the algorithm be ever in our favour,

Mariya Spektor
Director of Content, Social Chain

Dear Social Media Manager,

It's not rocket science nor open heart surgery. Everyone and their mom think they can do this job. But no, they can't. Not properly at least.

You've probably grown up with or directly on social media.
You know how trends work, how to hook the viewer, what formats work for organic reach, what formats work for community building and lead nurturing, how to make the report show nice numbers and how to make the stakeholders happy…

But social media as a channel tends to focus on those technical aspects, and not on the massive impact it can have on people's lives. How it forms opinions, emotions, relationships and among other things: self-perception.

Marketing often gets this negative stigma, that we use human nature for gain. And that messes with your head. Makes you question things and career choices. I know it did for me and mine.

But it doesn't have to be like that.

Don't get blinded by sales metrics. Don't get swayed into creating content that sells. Don't post CTAs and links in every post and story. Don't set KPIs based on industry benchmarks.

And for the love of everything nice and lovely - DO NOT try to increase followers as the main KPI. If someone asks you to do this - run the other way!

Aim to provide value.
Try to make the lives of your audience 10% better. Heck, even 2% would be great. Create relatable content. Make the problems, struggles and non-polished reality of your followers seen and heard, and people will organically gravitate towards your content.

And you'll increase those followers and sales numbers as a byproduct.

Focus on 'social', not just 'media'.

I believe in you. You've got this.

Mark Valasik
Creator of Marketing Right Side Up Youtube channel and Newsletter

Dear Social Media Manager,

The truth about socials is that they're always changing. Across eight of the major platforms, there are almost daily updates with new features, algorithm tweaks, and changes. And as social media becomes more embedded into the fabric of society; political, cultural and economic elements start to impact the social media world more & more. This creates more trends, cultural nuances and shifts in user behaviour, so staying informed and remaining agile is vital to stay relevant and drive engagement.

This means it's vital to keep experimenting with content & finding 1% marginal gains across platforms. However, it's also important to stay true to the underlying principles that make high-quality content. Because what truly drives performance is content that people want to share with their friends, screenshot, save for later, and genuinely find funny, valuable, or inspirational. High-**quality** content that resonates always will lead to high-**performing** content, especially in the long run.

As a social media manager, it can be easy to focus on the numbers and forget about the wider picture. Remember that your work on socials is there to drive tangible business outcomes & a bigger cause somewhere else. The more you understand how content & socials tie to the revenue of a business, the better you'll be at your job.

Matt Swain
CEO & Founder of Triangle

"The more you understand how content & socials tie to the revenue of a business, the better you'll be at your job."

Dear Social Media Manager,

I'm sure you've noticed things seem to change a lot when it comes to social media marketing. Every day it seems like someone's touting a new platform, a new strategy, a new tactic, and suggesting that theirs is the latest game-changer you should adopt and employ.

Don't fall for that trap.

It's a trap because these new "opportunities" are untested and unreliable. It's a trap because they haven't been weighed against your existing strategy. It's a trap because the hype and adrenaline are real, but the benefits aren't.

Yes, it's fun and exciting to try new things and be on the leading edge, particularly when it comes to social media marketing. And on the flip-side, it doesn't feel very good to see other brands, particularly competitors, capitalize on trends.

However, the old axiom is also true: the grass is always greener on the other side.

When we see others have success on a new platform or with a new tactic, we don't see all of the failures that led up to that moment, nor do we have the ability to discern their true business results at the end of the day, month or year.

To put it another way: can you recall a single brand whose ice bucket challenge video went viral, and their business benefited from it?

Because the truth is, your time and your brand's resources are finite. Instead of chasing new networks and fleeting fads, it's a far better investment of your time to focus on crafting an ironclad strategy for achieving actual business results from social media, and stick to it. Be mindful of the latest developments in social media, of course, and consider incorporating those options that seem to fit well with your marketing strategy and business needs, and ignore the rest.

Focus on using social media to create real connections with your audience and the latest developments will often be irrelevant.

Cheers,

Mike Allton
Consultant, Speaker & Author at The Social Media Hat

Dear Social Media Manager,

I am going to be brutally honest with you. Starting as a rookie in this industry took work. The amount of anxiety I got from LinkedIn in the first two weeks was insane. *One thing I wish I had known sooner* was that this industry is not a competition. It's a community. And having a community mindset is the first step in doing your job like a pro. You know, just because everybody is using social media, that doesn't mean that your role as a Social Media Manager is simple, easy, and ordinary. That is the biggest misconception about this job.

Now that we're talking about this role more seriously, let me share a few things I've observed and feel have not been discussed enough. Plus, I've found some solutions for myself that can work for you, too.

1. **Planning and creating content is not a lottery.** You can't just follow a trend and expect miracles. What the data says is actually what your audience is telling you. The type of content they prefer should be the content you create.

Tip: Spend some time understanding the metrics. Play with analytics on your platforms and look for patterns, differences, and missing pieces. Then, but only after all of this, let your creativity sparkle.

2. **Be cautious of external factors.** I'm talking about pop culture events, holidays, etc. And if you spend a lot of time on social media (and you probably do), you'll see that some things, such as sounds, words, and gestures, are susceptible to others, even if they are viral.

Tip: Make a calendar where you note every event monthly and whether it drew your attention (good or bad) on social media and might affect you (positively or negatively).

3. **Being a "stalker" was not part of the job requirements.** But you have to know your audience to the fullest because relatable content is king.

Tip: Follow your audience everywhere, on competitors' pages or different communities. I spend at least one-hour daily reading their comments. I copy-paste some of them into a sheet and highlight words I find useful. This way, you can use their words, feelings, and thoughts. Your content should be about them, not you or your brand.

So, take a deep breath, grab a coffee (or a matcha latte if that's your vibe), and HAVE FUN! Because you know what? In the end, this is what we all should do in our jobs (and life).

Your digital bestie,

Miruna Vocheci
Social Media Manager at Socialinsider.

Dear Social Media Manager

Dear Social Media Manager,

I am writing to you today to share my thoughts on the world of social media, where we have the opportunity to share the things we like and have a say on the things we dislike. This can make it an amazing, yet divisive, place. Because we're ALL very different.

It's important that we understand that when trying to create a community. Speak like a human being. Don't talk like a business. People relate to people.

Remain politically impartial but have your own values that people can align with and feel a part of. Don't push your personal views on others. Allow your followers a space to interact with you in a safe space without judgement. This is a two-way thing.

And then… be consistent with it. For ten years, we've set a creative brief every weekday. We've seen the community grow around the world because it's naturally inclusive and puts everyone on a level playing field. Whatever level they are at, or whoever they are, they are welcome to get involved to improve their creativity, contacts and overall wellbeing.

Navigating the ever-changing world, and the societal issues it brings, can be challenging. Do you play it safe or say what you really want to say? It's a fine-line but there's no in between. Know what you stand for and stick by it. But be prepared to get it wrong sometimes. We're only human.

With that, comes a need for resilience. Sometimes we try things that don't work or that people don't like. We live, we learn and we can apply that experience to the next project we do.

The pressure of putting ourselves out there publicly, day in, day out can be huge. However, building a strong support network around you can be invaluable. Never be afraid to ask for help or to collaborate with others to achieve your goals.

This is social media. So be sociable. Talk to people. Ask the question. What's the best that could happen?

This approach has led to us being able to collectively achieve huge successes including beating Justin Bieber to Xmas Number 1 and bringing our WWF #WorldWithoutNature campaign into its 4th year, surpassing a billion impressions.

These things don't happen without the small efforts of our followers on social media, submitting their quick-fire ideas. Every single entry to our daily briefs is as valuable as the next. Yes, we have competition winners, but it's vital that EVERYONE feels seen.

Forget AI and all the gimmicks, social media will always be about human beings. They want to feel part of something and related to.

You have the best job in the world to be able to make people smile amongst the negativity we often see online. You have the power to break up their doom scroll. Make them laugh. Help them create. Inform them. Involve them.

If you enjoy sharing your content. Others will enjoy receiving and interacting with it.

Above all, don't forget to have fun. Keep it simple and social.

Yours Socially,
Nick Entwistle
Creative Director & Founder of @OneMinuteBriefs

Dear Social Media Manager,

The first time I was responsible for social media, I was working as a Marketing Specialist at a advertising technology company. The extent of social media management in my day job at the time involved little more than scheduling pre-selected Twitter content to publish three times a day—and four times on weekends. It was tedious, boring, and over-engineered; the photo filters, copy structure, and posting schedule I had to use left little to the imagination.

What I didn't realize was the value of the lessons I was learning as a social media manager, even when I was frustrated or bored. Here are three things that I wish I had known when I started my career in social media marketing; hopefully it will help you whether you're starting your career or are a seasoned professional...

1. **Social media is not a passive marketing channel**. It was once enough for brands just to be present on social media. Today, however, simply publishing content regularly is not enough! It never ceases to amaze me how many of my colleagues view social media marketing as little more than a box-ticking exercise - just publish *something* on social and that's enough. Quality matters, now than ever—and when I say "quality" I don't mean the cost producing the post. Some of the most engaging and successful content I've created has been reactive content, which shows that our brand is listening to our followers and cares what they think.

Audiences are drowning in content, which means two things: first, pushing out content for the sake of it, is likely to hurt your brand than help it. Secondly, it's the story that matters. Whether you're telling a story in a single post or across a series, your audience will only take the action you want them to take if you succeed in storytelling.

2. **Draw inspiration from everything.** Today, I work for a company that produces mass spectrometers. Even though we sit in the B2B space, my colleagues and I take our inspiration not from other B2B companies, but from B2C consumer-facing companies that have spent years studying and testing what works when marketing to individual consumers.

One thing I tell everyone who joins my team: at the end of the day, we're selling mass spectrometers to *individuals*... who work for companies or organizations. We need to engage individuals the same way B2C companies do, particularly on social where we're fighting for every bit of attention.

3. **A career in social media is what you make of it.** Don't limit yourself to what's been done before. Success in social media means constant innovation, ideation, testing, and optimisation. Unlike some more traditional marketing channels, social media is rife with opportunities, and it's one area of outbound marketing that allows for true creativity.

With content creation on one side, execution and metrics on the other, social media managers must possess an array of skills—that's why no two social media experts are alike. If you enjoy data and drawing conclusions, as a social media manager you can do just that. Is storytelling more your forte? Then that's how you'll command your audience's attention.

To summarize, if there is only one thing I can impress upon you, dear Social Media Manager, it's this: social media is not a box that you need to fit into; but you can use it to create anything you can imagine, and those of you that are able to run with that will be successful, no matter what you to do.

Paige F. MacGregor
Senior Specialist, Brand & Social Media at SCIEX

Dear Social Media Manager,

If there's one thing that my decade-long journey in social media has taught me, it's that adaptability and continuous learning are... FUNDAMENTAL. (*A hint for my fellow RuPaul's Drag Race lovers*). Transitioning from dynamic advertising agencies to a tech company was a challenge but it showed me firsthand how fostering a culture of knowledge sharing and innovation is key to becoming better communicators and better colleagues.

In both tech and social media, there is a shared sense of innovation that comes from dedicating time to learning, experimenting, and creating.

For example, last year, we've started looking into the trending meme format to boost engagement. By understanding the humour and applying our brand's voice, we created content that not only worked with our community but also reached a wider audience, increasing not only followers but our overall engagement.

On the other hand, in social media, we are required to have a wide skillset—from data analytics to design and editing, copywriting, storytelling, and strategic thinking, the list could continue… and it can be tiring to check all the boxes.

It isn't easy to excel as a Social Media Manager as it involves mastering a diverse set of skills, but it's also very exciting to bring it all together and create a clear vision by understanding your brand and knowing how to get there.

But remember, you are not alone. The power of community through social media groups and networking with colleagues from different sectors, backgrounds, and markets cannot be overstated. Engaging in these spaces allows us to gain perspective, exchange ideas, stay current with trends, and form valuable connections that foster both personal growth and professional development.

A few months ago, we noticed our reach decreased drastically, but we couldn't decipher why. I tried looking for news or press releases and found nothing. Until I crossed paths with a post by a peer who was struggling with the same problem and helped us understand that it was an overall feeling, and we weren't alone in this.

My biggest tip is for you to nourish yourself with as much culture and knowledge as possible as it enriches you while allowing you to continuously add value to your work and the projects you're involved in.

To every Social Media Manager out there, I know it can be challenging, but there is a lot of value in what we do. While it requires immense time and dedication, some sleepless nights, the return and the sense of community is invaluable. I promise you; it is worth it!

You've got this!

Patricia Fernandes
Social Media Specialist at Mercedes-Benz.io

Dear Social Media Manager,

Welcome to one of the most exciting roles on the planet. It's been ten whole years of me working in this industry and *wow*, what a whirlwind it's been!

When I first started, social media was the wild west. You were lucky to be taken seriously if you had 'social media' in your job title. Now it's an extremely lucrative and rewarding career.

In recent years there's been a fantastic, very full-on shift in our industry. I hosted social media meetups between 2018 - 2020, connecting Social Media Managers together in central London. I loved it - meeting new people, chatting about working in social media, sharing stories, it was incredible! The sentiment around that time was that there weren't enough opportunities like that around, it could sometimes feel like a lonely career.

During the pandemic, this shifted. There are more opportunities than ever to meet fellow Social Media Managers in person - including whole conferences dedicated to social media. It's fantastic, whether you want to share your insights on stage, or learn from your peers, and even make new friends along the way! It can also be *incredibly* daunting. We're in an era of being *on* all the time. I love it - but it comes at a cost. The realm of boundaries between work and play are more blurred than ever before, and I truly think that's one of the most difficult things about this industry. It can make it feel very hard to hold yourself to the same standards on social media, that you might hold a client. It might even make you 'notification blind' - yes, I am terrible at responding to WhatsApp's (sorry friends, don't take it personally!) but that comes with the territory. There was even a Christmas one year when I decided I would have a social media holiday. I removed all the apps from my phone, leaving only Reddit as I didn't think that counted. Note to self, it does count - but the sentiment was there!

This industry changes at the drop of a hat. Social media platforms come and go. You have to be prepared to rewrite a social media strategy at the drop of a hat - coffee becomes your best friend to help you power through. It can feel gruelling at times - but the rewards are worth it. I tell you one thing - the industry might change frequently, but the support is *strong*, more so in the last year or so. It feels like there's a buzz in the air, everyone is eager, people are genuinely excited and passionate about the future of our industry.

Let's see what the future of social media holds - together!

Rebecca Holloway
Senior Social Media Strategist at Base Creative

Dear Social Media Manager

Dear, Social Media Manager,

Welcome to the lion's den. A little wild, a little like Aslan; but very bold and daring. "A medium that is always in a state of flux." Push and pull, push and pull; social media is a constant tug of war between chaos, clarity, approvals and, sometimes hitting the jackpot of creating delightful moments. But take your social veneers off for a second and let's talk…

Let's start with this…

…you bring a lot of horsepower to the team. Don't let anyone ever tell you otherwise. You are a melting pot of creativity, community and connections. Storytelling is in your DNA, and you can sniff an unmet market need at the click of a cursor. You thrive on building communities that connect and convert; and you are always fluid: sometimes capitalizing on trends and sometimes setting them.

Remember, that at the end of the day, you will always make it to the checkered flag because it's all about testing and learning. Don't try to race anyone, and don't operate from a place of comparison. Growth takes time, but you keep operating with speed till you find a sweet spot. Why? Because while you can't plan virality, you can plan mentality. Over the years you will ride the many algo-rhythmic waves, and you will develop both muscle memory and scar tissue. That's normal. You will feel the pressure to move at the speed of culture. You will fight many battles with leadership on creating content that entertains and educates vs content that
hyper focuses on the product. Sometimes you'll win that battle, and other times you won't. Don't get demoralized. The community never lies, and the numbers will eventually do all the talking. Save your energy.

My advice to you is to always observe, absorb, extract and

transform. Have a debugging mentality, and remind yourself that sometimes it's OKAY to venture off, steer back (if needed) and find new paths to relay the same message in creative ways. Never just operate off of a feeling - lean into data. Benchmark consistently, but also find ways to show up in non-traditional ways. Social media marketing is not about rinsing and repeating what is working for other brands. It's also about finding your own footing. Advocate for yourself, talk about your work, and get sponsorship from leaders who
will take your name in a room full of executive influence. That is your key to getting leadership buy-in.

But remember, if you ever feel boxed; like your creative spark is dying; it's okay to move on and find a new home. Don't ever try to jam a square peg in a round hole. Go somewhere your superpowers are appreciated. It might take time, but there's a place for everyone.

Keep going my braveheart,

Sabreen Haziq

Head of Marketing at Vista Social
Former Head of Global Social Media at Formlabs

Dear Social Media Manager,

First, well done on getting this far. You have chosen to do something worthwhile and potentially exciting with your life. Being a Social Media Manager is not an easy role. It requires many skills, namely: creativity, organisation, analysis, tenacity, communication, and sales prowess.

The key skill which runs through the whole process of being a social media manager is communication. Yes, communicating the client's brand message, their products, or services etc to the world at large. What I want to focus on here, however, is the communication between you, the Social Media Manager, and your client. This begins before you even agree to start working together.

Right from an initial meeting with a prospective client, it's important to clearly communicate the services you offer and, just as importantly, those which you don't. Managing client expectations is key at every step, never more so than at the beginning. Social media managers all work in different ways; having clear communication will help the client journey move much more smoothly and will be more enjoyable for all parties.

Sharing your initial creative ideas with your client is a great way to ensure you're not going down the wrong path. Presenting an outline strategy before you delve into detail will give your client a feeling of being involved in the process as well as potentially saving you a lot of wasted time.

Monthly meetings with clients are important. Sometimes they may just feel like a nice chat, but what you're doing is eliciting information which you can use for content for the month ahead. Clients sometimes don't see that an event or occasion is relevant. If you're relying on email or a list of questions, they may not mention it, whereas a more comfortable or casual conversation may lead someone to reveal more. You may find out that it's someone's birthday or that they've taken on a new member of staff or, as with one client I worked with recently, the white paper which the company had been working on for months, was ready to be published! I would have been so cross if I hadn't known about that!

Finally, it's vital in an ongoing client relationship to lay boundaries. Communicating when you are available – and when you're not – could save many awkward moments. There will always be clients who want you to make changes at the last minute. If you have communicated clearly up front, these situations can be managed to your benefit. This will happen much less if a) a client has seen the posting schedule in advance and b) if they're aware that a fee will be charged for late changes.

So, while you're in charge of the outward communication of the company on their social media, don't underestimate the power and importance of internal communications between the client and yourself.

Enjoy the process and have fun – being a social media manager can lead you into places you never knew existed! Embrace the journey!

Sarah Clay
CEO of Sarah Clay Social

Dear Social Media Manager,

To the outside world, the work of Social Media Managers looks exciting and glamorous. Getting paid to do IG all day sounds fun!

But those on the inside know it's rarely like that. Instead, it's:
- nonstop deadlines.
- never-ending content updates.
- ever-changing algorithms.
- bosses who know little about the work but care disproportionately about the results.
- colleagues who think "the social media guy/gal can just push it out."
- constant exposure to trolls, attacks, ugly responses.
- a high-wire act with no safety net.

On top of all that, pay for social media managers is typically less than what they deserve. Many should be getting cyber-combat pay for all they go through. All are frontline workers in today's digital-first world.

So why do I still train, coach and hire folks for such roles? Because being a Social Media Manager is a chance to:
- do more meaningful work at earlier points in your career than expected.
- represent and speak for your company or nonprofit on a daily basis.
- interact with, even coach, C-suite leaders.
- learn skills that will last you a lifetime.

Finally, since you won't hear it often enough, I'll just say: THANK YOU!

Sree Sreenivasan
CEO at Digimentors

"Pay for social media managers is typically less than what they deserve."

Dear Social Media Manager,

As a former Social Media Manager, I understand the unique blend of creativity, strategy, and resilience the role demands. It has constantly evolved over the last 10 years and is both exhilarating and challenging, and I'd like to share some insights and reflections from my own journey.

What I Wish I Knew Before Starting:
Entering the social media industry, I was prepared for fast-paced changes but underestimated the importance of adaptability. Platforms evolve rapidly—consider the rise of TikTok, which saw its monthly active users surpass 1.5 billion in early 2024. Staying current with trends is vital, but so is understanding the underlying algorithms that drive engagement and reach.

General Tips and Advice:
Stay Informed: Regularly update your knowledge with the latest trends and algorithm changes. Tools like HubSpot, Hootsuite, and SproutSocial offer excellent resources.

Analytics is your new best friend: Use data to drive decisions and seek opportunities. In 2024, the average engagement rate for brands on Instagram is 1.16%, according to Social Media Today. Understanding metrics like these helps in tailoring strategies and builds authority to your audience.

Balance Creativity with Consistency: While innovative content is crucial, maintaining a consistent posting schedule is equally important. A well-planned content calendar can make a significant difference - however make sure you keep an open-mind, news happens anytime of the day so be prepared to create a post in an instant.

Views on the Role and Industry: Our roles are often misunderstood. We are strategists, analysts, and content creators rolled into one. This multifaceted nature is what makes our job exciting yet demanding. The industry itself is dynamic—recent trends show an increasing emphasis on authenticity and user-generated content, with 79% of consumers preferring brands that share genuine stories and with the rise of AI, who can blame them.

Enjoyment and Challenges: What I enjoyed most about working in social media is the opportunity to engage with a diverse audience and make a tangible impact. Crafting a campaign that resonates with an audience and the client can be incredibly rewarding. However, the pressure to constantly produce engaging content and the challenge of managing online negativity are significant hurdles. It's important to set boundaries and manage work/life balance effectively otherwise this role will get a little more difficult for you.

Constructive Challenges: One of the major challenges are the algorithm changes. For example, in 2024, Facebook's algorithm prioritises content that sparks meaningful interactions. While this encourages quality engagement, it can also be a double-edged sword, making it harder to achieve organic reach. The key is to focus on creating value-driven content that encourages interaction and community building.

Conclusion: To all my fellow social media managers, remember that our work is impactful. Stay curious, keep learning, and support each other in this wonderful field. Together, we can navigate the highs and lows and continue to drive innovation in the social media landscape.

Best regards,

Tania Gerard
Founder at Tania Gerard Digital
Dear Social Media Manager,

I started social media managing during college where Twitter and Instagram were the new platforms. We went from sharing photos of our lunches to live tweeting and streaming from events and trending hashtags, etc. By the time COVID lockdown came along in 2020, it was a job that paid majority of my bills. This is when I started to teach social media etiquette and safety protocols for minors online. Allow me to share some pointers:

Common Mistakes:
- Oversharing: private information like our whereabouts, full birthdates, etc.

- Impulse control: with the immediate access to information and getting what we need when we want it, we can share and express ourselves fast. That is not a great idea as there is no such thing as delete when it comes to the internet. So, if you bad mouth someone online, it could tarnish your reputation.

Cons of Social Media:
- As previously mentioned, we don't own what we put out there online. The platforms do, so people are learning the hard way how social media is a tool that is not controllable.

- Advertising and manipulation from shopping to voting habits have been proven and still legal. The law is always behind the technology, so you have to be aware of just how much you share and why the ads you are being targeted.

- The growth of mental health disorders. There is so much information, and it is impossible to be on top of it all. Along with the growth of plastic surgery due to filters and cyberbullying because it continues past the school doors.

Pros of Social Media:
- Growth in understanding on previously social stigmas like

depression, sexual orientation and other social issues allowed for things to come to light. An example is the Me Too Movement where women from all over the world shared that they were sexually harassed at some point in their life simply by putting #MeToo. It was news to many men, not realizing the constant harassment women go through on a daily basis.

- Finding a community that was previously inaccessible. Even in remote parts of the world, people, especially minors, such as as members of the LGBTQ+ community or someone with a learning difficulty can find a community online.

Before I end, here are some helpful tips:
- Be aware of your settings, particularly what apps have access to your microphone, camera and location. Rarely does an app need to have access "even when not using."

- Establish a healthy digital rule but be reasonable. For instance, do not allow your phone near your bed or turn off notifications, especially during non-work hours.

- Remember, don't say anything online you wouldn't want your grandmother to see. I always say, a diary was never meant to be public.

Social media has its uses, but it is our duty to navigate and use our best judgement as managers for our own and our clients content. We have a responsibility, and we will screw up but when you understand this and take it seriously, a lot of good can happen. I hope this was useful. See you online.

Best,
Tara Jabbari
Digital Media Consultant

Dear Social Media Manager,

People say that everyone should do a stint working in hospitality (I've been there, done that) but the corporate world edition is; everyone should work in social media at a point in their careers. I believe it will teach you more about yourself than many other industries could. You will learn skills quicker, learn to understand human behaviour, all whilst growing a thick skin too. It wouldn't surprise me if in the future, a lot of CMO's and CEO's have once worked in social.

So, let's get in to it, the good, bad and the ugly of social media…

Working in social media can be an incredibly lonely place, especially if you find yourself as a team of 1. You have no peer support, no sounding board and nobody that just 'gets it' and let me tell you, that's something you need. You may feel burnt out at times from the nature of always needing to be 'on'. You will find yourself trying to stay up to date with the latest news, trends and platforms in social media, because if you don't know these things– you fall behind with best practices in the industry. I often wonder if there's any other job you have to be ready to change how you work on daily basis, because that's our reality as Social Media Managers. Being adaptable at such a frequent pace, is something we should all be incredibly proud of, so give yourself a pat on the back.

You might be somebody who finds yourself caught up in 8 rounds of approvals and 'going through legal' for just one post (hello regulated industries). How about getting told you're the worst human on earth and several expletives by *Ethel and her 10 cats all before 9am and your morning coffee? You're also trying to get the balance right in taking time off social media in your personal time, but that seems like an impossible task in itself. Then there's the lack of understanding of social media from stakeholders which Social Media Managers face time and time again. Not to mention the 'post this' (non-social optimised content) or 'can you make it go viral' questions – this is not a circus, although maybe sometimes it is?

We also can't speak about the bad side of social without mentioning the widespread low salaries in the social media industry, that are benchmarked against each other. If CEO's and CMO's did one week working in social media, they would give every single Social Media Manager a raise. However, this isn't 'Undercover Boss', so try and get your C-suite execs to a social media conference, so they can get a better understanding of the industry. If you can't do that (and even if you can), get them a copy of this book, because it will change their perspective or at least here's hoping it does.

So, with all that being said, why do I ~~like~~ love working in social media?

I believe working in social media excels your professional growth unlike any other corporate job from entry-level jobs upwards. The skillset you learn through social media can be applied to various tasks, roles and even other industries, including becoming highly adaptable because you pivot constantly. We are failing faster because there's always things to learn and being somebody who's willing to do that, is actually quite a rare commodity in today's day and age when so many people are stuck in their ways.

You learn the art of patience and to not take things personally. You're good at ideation, pitching, creating, experimenting, data collecting, analysing insights, reiterating, testing (again) and you understand the psychology of marketing, whilst being able to claim a person's attention, whom is passively scrolling with the attention span of a nat.

There aren't many jobs out there where you get to be both creative and analytical and where no day is the same even when you're doing repetitive tasks. These are two of my favourite things about working in social media.

Like many industries, it isn't all sunshine and rainbows but with the right community around you IRL, online and in the form of this book, even on the challenging days, working in social is both a fun and fulfilling career.

Wherever you are in your career or knowledge of social media, as long as you're willing to learn, you'll be just fine.

I hope to see you online or in-person at an event soon.

Xandrina Allday
Author of Dear Social Media Manager
Founder of Social Retreats
Social Media Manager at LabX Media Group

*Ethel and her 10 cats are fictional characters, as to encompass all the many trolls and people we encounter on a daily basis across social media.

Contributors

Adina Jipa is a marketer with 14 years experience in digital marketing. She left behind her 9-to-5 job as a product marketer to embark on a new journey – building her own product. Socialinsider combines social intelligence, analytics, and listening into one single tool.
https://www.socialinsider.io/

Alexus Brittain has been a dynamic presence in social media management since 2020, starting with B2C content creation for smaller agencies. Currently, she is the head of social media at Vista Social, where she has excelled in B2B marketing for the past two years.
https://www.linkedin.com/in/alexus-brittain-5105b4154/

Andrea Kilin is a versatile marketing and communications expert. With a decade of experience, she blends creative flair with data prowess, and known for leading dynamic social media strategies and championing diversity and inclusion.
https://www.linkedin.com/in/kilinandrea/

Anna Bertoldini is the Senior Social Media Influencer and Brand Manager at NielsenIQ. She is focused on strengthening NIQ's brand story across social, reinforcing the organization's thought leadership, and amplifying its global voice through social advocacy and influencer and brand partnerships.
https://www.linkedin.com/in/annabertoldini

Anna Wamsler started working in social media in 2017, prior to this she was a journalist. Currently, she is a Social Media Manager, she is also a Social Media Expert at Mitteldeutscher Rundfunk, which is part of German public service broadcasting.
www.linkedin.com/in/anna-wamsler

Anthony Leung is a business consultant and LinkedIn marketing specialist committed to helping brands and business leaders create authentic written and video content for LinkedIn. Drawing on his extensive experience with top brands like JUST EAT and Pret, Anthony offers over a decade of expertise in social media strategy and content creation.
https://www.linkedin.com/in/meanwritehook/

Carolyn Campbell-Baldwin is an experienced digital marketing expert specialising in Pinterest strategies for sustainable travel brands. With extensive experience living and working abroad, Carolyn leverages her multilingual skills and global insights to help travel businesses increase their visibility and website traffic.
https://www.linkedin.com/in/carolyncampbell-baldwin/

Corrie Jones has 10+ years in the social media industry and 6 years running her own social media agency which she sold in 2022. In that time, she's had the joy of working on award-winning projects with brands like NatWest, Virgin StartUp, and Cancer Research to name a few. She now leads the savvy social media team at StrategiQ, the global value creation agency.
https://www.linkedin.com/in/corriejones/

Dave Endsor is a UK-based marketing and social media specialist with nearly 15+ years experience in agency and in-house marketing.
daveendsor.com

Diana Rapine has over 5 years of experience in social media, holds an MBA and is the owner of Palm + Pine Marketing and Design. She's passionate about creating content and helping brands grow, she specialises in social media for a diverse range of e-commerce brands.
www.palmpine.design

Dynamitri Joachim Nawrot has 16 years working in the social media industry, he's been around since early Facebook and Twitter days: specialised in the music industry, worked with automotive, tech, telco, beauty, sports, charities, childcare and personal training, too, amongst others. He tackles impossibilities straight away, with miracles take a little more time.
https://www.linkedin.com/in/dynamitri/

Emma Glover is the founder and social media lead at Nottingham-based agency, Victress Digital. She's managed the accounts of Kellogg's South Africa, Dulux, and Barclays Africa, and worked as the lead social advertising strategist on multi-million dollar SaaS brands.
https://victressdigital.co.uk/

Fab Giovanetti is an award-winning author, entrepreneur and marketer of 15 years. She is the CEO of Alt Marketing School, looking to make marketing more impactful, accessible, inclusive and fun. Featured in The Next Web, Business Insider, Forbes among others, she was nominated one of the 50 digital women to watch in 2023 and 2022. She was also recognised among the top 100 Marketers in 2023 by Growth Daily and one of the Top 100 Marketing Influencers Index 2023.
https://fabgiovanetti.com

Grace Clemens is a seasoned marketing professional of 13 years, she specialises in digital marketing audits for e-commerce brands, bringing a unique perspective to discussions around marketing. Her expertise lies in crafting and executing multi-channel marketing strategies that drive revenue and foster meaningful audience engagement.
gracieclemens.com.

Grace McLaughlin is a South Jersey native turned California girl, she brings over 10 years of marketing expertise to the table. Her expertise lies in social media, content creation, athlete management, and event planning, especially for e-commerce and active lifestyle brands. Grace's favourite part of the job? Creating genuine connections and getting creative!
https://www.linkedin.com/in/josephteols/

Gus Bhandal is a highly-experienced Marketing Strategist and Social Media Specialist. In 2017, he founded 'The M Guru' – a digital marketing agency supporting business owners how to maximise social media (especially LinkedIn) for long-term, sustainable growth.
https://www.linkedin.com/in/mguruuk

Holly Hammond is currently the Social Media Coordinator at the online science publication, Technology Networks. Having found social media through some winding paths, she leans into the creative opportunities the landscape provides. Outside of social media, she can probably be found with animals, in nature, or gaming.
https://www.linkedin.com/in/hollyghammond

James Erskine has worked in marketing for 25 years, the last 15 of those being in social media. He is a serial entrepreneur and created the UK's first commercial podcast network and the UK's first influencer marketing agency. He is currently CEO of Rocket a best-in-class youth and family marketing agency focussed on social media.
https://www.linkedin.com/in/jameserskine

Joe Teo is the CEO of HeyOrca - the social media scheduler for that's perfect for teams. He started HeyOrca in 2016 when he saw a need for a collaborative solution for social media teams. When he's not helping social media teams take back their days, you can catch him deep in thought, pondering the existential questions of life. Also, he's in his dad era and appreciates a well-manicured lawn.
https://www.linkedin.com/in/josephteols/

Jonathan Hatch got his start in social media in 2011 when he left the medical field. He is current Global Talent Brand Manager at Zoom, previously the former Social Media Manager at Florida Blue and Digital Marketing Manager over Social at Availity, and Director Paid Social at SeaWorld Parks and Entertainment. When he's not cooking up marketing campaigns, he enjoys staying active, traveling, and keeping up with his two Siberian huskies, Ash and Denali.
www.linkedin.com/in/jonathanghatch

Karla McNeilage was formerly the Head of Social Media for various e-commerce businesses. Karla is now the founder of her own business, Wave Socials. She has worked in the industry for 8 years and now uses her expertise and experience to drive growth, particularly focusing on making brands memorable through story-led marketing strategies.
https://www.linkedin.com/in/karlamcneilage/

Kate Berry is a highly experienced social media strategist, currently working in the life science industry. With a robust background in social media spanning over 8 years, she has honed her expertise through both in-house and agency roles.
https://www.linkedin.com/in/kate-e-berry/

Katie Murphy is a Social Media Manager based in Manchester, UK with a passion for making the world a better place by talking about things she cares about, all while being a little bit silly.
https://www.linkedin.com/in/katie-murphy-b79ba8129/

Kim Stavropoulos is a word enthusiast, she may be short, but she packs a powerful punch. Her energy, enthusiasm, and dedication to digital content and social media know no bounds. Passionate about strategy, content marketing, and the occasional pop culture reference, she thrives on connecting and collaborating to produce excellence.
https://www.linkedin.com/in/kimstavropoulos/

Lauren Grubb is a Social Media Executive at StrategiQ Marketing. With three years of experience in the marketing world, she works across a number of clients and industries to create social media content, build communities and help businesses thrive. Lauren is passionate about sharing her knowledge and insights through university webinars and actively developing her personal brand on LinkedIn.
https://www.linkedin.com/in/lauren-grubb-104127184/

Lena Weber-Reed is a Social Media Strategist steering startups, scale-ups, and global brands through the evolving social media landscape. As a pioneer, she thrives on being the first social media marketer on the ground, building strategies from the ground up. Lena currently lives in Glasgow, Scotland, with her family and pet entourage.
https://www.linkedin.com/in/lenaweberreed

Magali Mas D'Amato is a Marketing Consultant specialising in social media. She has over 7 years of experience helping international companies grow their online presence.
https://www.linkedin.com/in/magalimasdamato/

Maja Ivić was born and raised in Sarajevo, the capital city of a small Balkan country, Bosnia and Herzegovina. After completing her master's in Journalism, she moved to Germany, where she lived for over seven years. Currently, she resides in Krakow, Poland. Her multicultural background has given her a unique perspective on consumer behaviour across different markets. She believes in creating genuine connections through content that speaks to the audience's heart.
https://www.linkedin.com/in/majaivic/

Mandie Geller's unique blend of a photography background and journalism degree creates the perfect recipe for an engaging and impactful social media career. She currently is the Head of Social & Photography for a restaurant group in San Diego, California.
https://www.linkedin.com/in/mandie-geller-802493b6/

Mandy Karl, from Southwestern, ON, has enriched the social media marketing landscape for over a decade. A freelance artist, avid volunteer, and musician, she brings creativity and passion to every endeavour.
https://www.linkedin.com/in/mandykarl/

Marianne Avery supports solopreneurs and small businesses to thrive on LinkedIn™, helping them master the power of the platform to grow their network and their business. Through a combination of training, audits, and personalised coaching, she'll create a winning LinkedIn™ profile and strategy that attracts their ideal clients and gets them on side.
https://www.linkedin.com/in/marianneavery/

Mariya Spektor is a creative leader with over eight years of experience in social media strategies, content creation, and driving millions of engagements across multiple platforms. She has worked across both agency and in-house, on clients such as TikTok, Afterpay, and more!
https://www.linkedin.com/in/mariyaspektor/

Mark Valasik is the creator of marketing Youtube channel and Newsletter MarketingRightSideUp.com. He was the former CMO at Social Media Management tool for Social Media Managers Kontentino.
https://www.linkedin.com/in/valasik/

Matt Swain has had a variety of roles in socials working with some of the UK's most influential figures, managing accounts with over 1 million followers, judging national social media awards and creating the world's most exclusive social media community, Social Club. Matt is Founder & CEO of Triangle, a branding agency working with UK & US leading entrepreneurs and is also an International Speaker.
www.mattswain.com

Mike Allton is a Strategic Marketing Leader in AI and Data-Driven Solutions at The Social Media Hat, host of the AI in Marketing: Unpacked podcast, international keynote speaker & author, and Head of Strategic Partnerships at Agorapulse where he strengthens relationships with social media educators, influencers and partner brands. He has spent over a decade in digital marketing and brings an unparalleled level of experience and excitement to the fore, whether he's delivering a presentation or leading a workshop.
www.TheSocialMediaHat.com

Miruna Vocheci graduated with an M.A. in Content and Media Strategy and a B.A. in Journalism. She is currently the Social Media Manager at SocialInsider and loves to catch trends, read nerdy things about Media Studies, and spot semiotics signs everywhere.
https://www.linkedin.com/in/miruna-vocheci/

Nick Entwistle is the Creative Director and Founder of the Bank of Creativity, working with agencies and brands to create compelling content to engage their audiences and generate big interest in their products or services. He is also the founder of our global user-generated content community, @OneMinuteBriefs, which has a client list featuring the likes of WWF, Twitter, Coca-Cola, Oxfam, Pringles, Adobe, PG Tips, KFC & Guinness.
https://linktr.ee/bankofcreativity

Paige F. MacGregor has nearly 15 years of experience studying and working in social media marketing. Currently, Paige works as Senior Specialist for Brand & Social Media at SCIEX, a Danaher Corporation operating company, where she is responsible for global social media marketing strategy and execution. Paige volunteers her free time and expertise to several nonprofit/not-for-profit organizations, including The Minority Report podcast, Single Mothers by Choice, and LibertyLand Axolotl Rescue.
https://www.linkedin.com/in/paigefmacgregor/

Patricia Fernandes has been a Social Media Manager since June 2015, she's now happily doing her thing at a tech company. "GLITTER & TEARS" is the first line of her Instagram bio, and it couldn't be more herself.
https://www.linkedin.com/in/patbfer/

Rebecca Holloway is an award-winning Senior Social Media Strategist & International Speaker with 10+ years of experience, specialising in strategy, thought leadership, and paid social within B2B sectors. Outside of social media, you'll find Rebecca in her garden planting sunflowers, or planning her next camping trip to the seaside.
https://www.linkedin.com/in/beccasocial/

Sabreen Haziq is a creative marketing leader with a demand generation bent of mind, and loves finding electric and unapologetic ways to connect brands with audiences though education that entertains. With 6 solid years in social media marketing, and with a specialized masters in Social Media Culture and Society from the University of Westminster, London; Sabreen has helped double unicorns scale their social into the millions! Outside of her current role as Head of Marketing at Vista Social, Sabreen is a podcast host of the premier self-improvement podcast called, The Lavender Fix.
https://www.linkedin.com/in/sabreenhaziq/

Sarah Clay is a LinkedIn trainer and consultant as well as CEO of Sarah Clay Social managing LinkedIn company pages for her B2B clients helping them get more reach across LinkedIn. Sarah is also a keynote speaker, published author and employee advocacy expert keeping #LinkedInSimplified with her no-nonsense, clear talking approach.
https://sarahclaysocial.com/

Sree Sreenivasan is CEO & cofounder of Digimentors, which offers social/digital/AI training and consulting. He served as chief digital officer of Columbia University, the Metropolitan Museum of Art and the City of New York.
http://linkedin.com/in/sreenivasan

Tania Gerard is an experienced digital marketing professional and former Head of Digital, where she developed expertise in social media strategy and creating engaging digital content. With over a decade of experience in social media management and digital marketing, Tania is now the Founder of Tania Gerard Digital, a company dedicated to promoting inclusivity through Neurodiversity in the Workplace workshops. Her passion for innovative digital solutions and commitment to fostering inclusive work environments make her a sought-after leader in the industry.
http://www.taniagerard.co.uk/

Tara Jabbari has worked in all aspects of digital media for over 10 years, from videos, and social media to podcasting working in over 5 countries. She concentrates on working with podcasters and organizations increase impact and become recognized experts, and ultimately exceed their initial expectations through digital marketing.
https://about.me/tarajabbari

Xandrina Allday is an industry award-winning International Speaker, Founder of Social Retreats, Social Media Manager at LabX Media Group and the Author of Dear Social Media Manager, her full bio can be read on the About the Author page.
https://uk.linkedin.com/in/socialmediatips

About The Author

Xandrina Allday is an award-winning International Social Media Speaker. She has spoken at industry leading social media conferences such as SocialDay and the International Social Media Summit. She has extensive experience training individuals and teams on the subjects of Social Media Strategy, Organic Social, Paid Social, Facebook, LinkedIn, AI in Social Media, Personal Branding, Employee Advocacy and more.

Xandrina is the Founder of Social Retreats, offering social media retreats to social media professionals and teams. She has been working across social media and marketing roles since 2015, currently leading the social media team and efforts for LabX Media Group brands.

She is happily engaged, raising her two daughters and renovating her home in the Suffolk countryside. Dear Social Media Manager is the first book authored by Xandrina and she hopes it will be the first of many. She can be reached on LinkedIn where she is an active part of the social media community.

Social Retreats

Retreats for social media professionals and teams.
Find out more, visit: www.socialretreats.co.uk

Printed in Great Britain
by Amazon